W9-CBD-734

[Visual] the Guide to Second Grade

Grade

2

Thinking Kids™
An imprint of Carson-Dellosa Publishing LLC
P.O. Box 35665
Greensboro, NC 27425 USA

Thinking Kids™
An imprint of Carson-Dellosa Publishing LLC
P.O. Box 35665
Greensboro, NC 27425 USA

Printed in the USA • All rights reserved.   ISBN 978-1-4838-2683-7
01-060167784

Infographics and Learning Activities

Welcome to Earth!

Earth is about 4.5 billion years old.

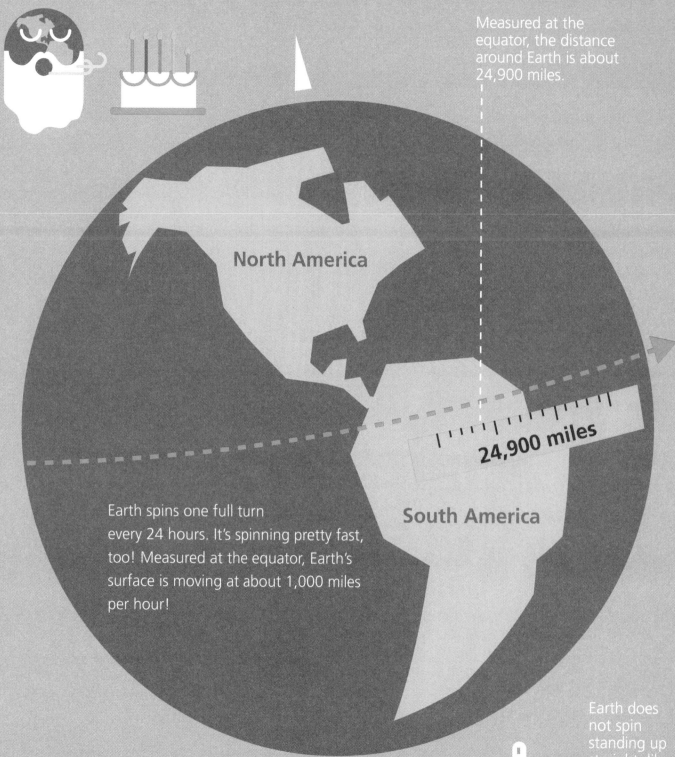

Measured at the equator, the distance around Earth is about 24,900 miles.

North America

24,900 miles

South America

Earth spins one full turn every 24 hours. It's spinning pretty fast, too! Measured at the equator, Earth's surface is moving at about 1,000 miles per hour!

Earth does not spin standing up straight, like a top. Instead, Earth tilts. That is why we have seasons.

Earth is the third planet from the Sun.

Earth weighs about

13,170,000,000,000,000,000,000,000

pounds!

Earth moves through space at 67,000 miles per hour. Even at that speed, it takes Earth one year to complete an orbit around the Sun.

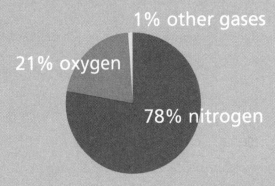

1% other gases

21% oxygen

78% nitrogen

The air on Earth is mostly made of nitrogen, not oxygen.

About 71% of Earth's surface is covered in water. The rest is land.

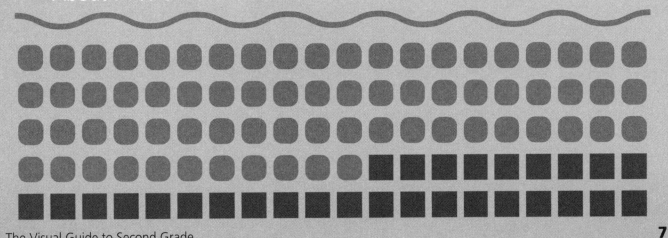

Make Pictographs

How old is Earth? Make a pictograph to show Earth's age. Use the key. Draw a globe for each one billion years of Earth's history.

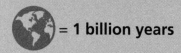 = **1 billion years**

How long does it take Earth to spin one full turn? Make a pictograph to show the time needed for the Earth to rotate. Use the key. Draw a clock for each hour.

 = **1 hour**

Read About It:
The Reason for the Seasons

WHY IS THE TEMPERATURE warm for part of the year and cold for the other part? The reason is Earth's tilt. The United States lies in the Northern Hemisphere, or the top half of Earth. For part of the year, this half of the planet is tilted toward the Sun. In the Northern Hemisphere, this part of the year is called *spring* and *summer*. The air feels warm then because the top half of Earth is closer to the Sun. During the part of the year when the top half of Earth is farther away from the Sun, it is *autumn* and *winter* in the Northern Hemisphere. In these months, the air feels much colder.

The bottom half of Earth is the Southern Hemisphere. Australia and other countries lie in this region. In the Southern Hemisphere, the seasons are opposite! During spring and summer in the United States, the bottom half of Earth is tilted away from the Sun. It is autumn and winter in Australia, and it is time to wear jackets and gloves. During autumn and winter in the Northern Hemisphere, the Southern Hemisphere is closer to the Sun. Then, people in Australia are wearing shorts and enjoying spring and summer temperatures.

Make a Chart

Read the passage above. Then, complete the chart. Write the seasons *Winter, Spring, Summer,* and *Autumn*, in order, for each hemisphere.

Months	Southern Hemisphere Season (Australia)	Northern Hemisphere Season (United States)
December, January, February		
March, April, May		
June, July, August		
September, October, November		

Goal!

Soccer is a favorite sport of kids around the world. You don't need much to play—just a ball, a few friends, and a lot of energy. The rules are easy to learn, but playing well takes practice. If you love soccer, you have something in common with millions of people around the globe!

In most parts of the world, soccer is called *football*.

In 1930, the first World Cup soccer tournament was held in South America.

In the Middle Ages, soccer balls were made from blown-up pigs' bladders!

Women have played soccer for hundreds of years.

Soccer players run about six miles during each game.

During the 1970s, women's soccer teams were formed around the world.

Mia Hamm

- known as the best American female soccer player of all time
- in 1991, helped the United States win the first Women's World Cup

with **158** goals, held the world record for most total goals in women's soccer for 14 years

Landon Donovan

- known as the best male American soccer player of all time
- helped his teams win 6 Major League Soccer championships

scored **144** goals during the years he played

Pelé

- known as the greatest male soccer player of all time
- helped his team, Brazil, win 3 World Cups

scored **1,281** goals during the years he played

Marta

- FIFA World Player of the Year for five years in a row: 2006 to 2010

has scored **15** goals during Women's World Cup matches—more than any other player!

More than 1 billion people count themselves as soccer fans!

Soccer is the most popular sport on Earth.

The World Cup is played every four years.

There are 11 players on each team in a soccer game.

In 1884, the American Football (Soccer) Association was started.

Professional soccer games are 90 minutes long.

Think and Solve

Study the infographic. Answer the questions.

1. What is soccer called in most countries around the world?

_____

2. True or false? Soccer is no longer the most popular sport in the world.

_____

3. In a professional soccer game, there are _____players on each team.
  A. 11
  B. 5
  C. 15
  D. 12

4. The World Cup is played every _____.
  A. two years
  B. four years
  C. six years
  D. eight years

Read About It: **The World Cup**

THE WORLD CUP IS THE MOST POPULAR SPORTING EVENT in the world. This soccer tournament takes place every four years. In 2014, the country of Brazil hosted the Men's World Cup. Thirty-two teams began the tournament. These teams were divided into eight groups of four. In each group, the two teams that scored the most goals advanced. The next round began with these 16 teams. These teams played each other in eight matches, and the winners went on to the next round. In 2014, the final eight teams were Brazil, Colombia, France, Germany, the Netherlands, Costa Rica, Argentina, and Belgium. These teams played each other, with the winner advancing from each match to the next round. In 2014, Germany was the final winner.

The Women's World Cup is also held every four years. It takes place one year after the men's. In 2015, Canada was the host. It was the biggest Women's World Cup ever, with 24 teams competing. In 2015, the final eight teams were China, the United States, Germany, France, Australia, Japan, England, and Canada. The United States was the final winner!

Piece It Together

Cut out the names of the final eight national soccer teams that competed in the 2015 Women's World Cup. Glue or tape them in the correct spaces to complete the bracket on page 15. A *bracket* shows which teams played each other in a tournament and which team won each game. The team in each pair that is in **bold** print is the winner of that match.

1 China

8 **Japan**

2 **USA**

9 Canada

3 **Germany**

10 **England**

4 France

11 **Japan**

5 **USA**

12 England

6 Germany

13 **USA**

7 Australia

14 Japan

15 USA

2015 Women's World Cup

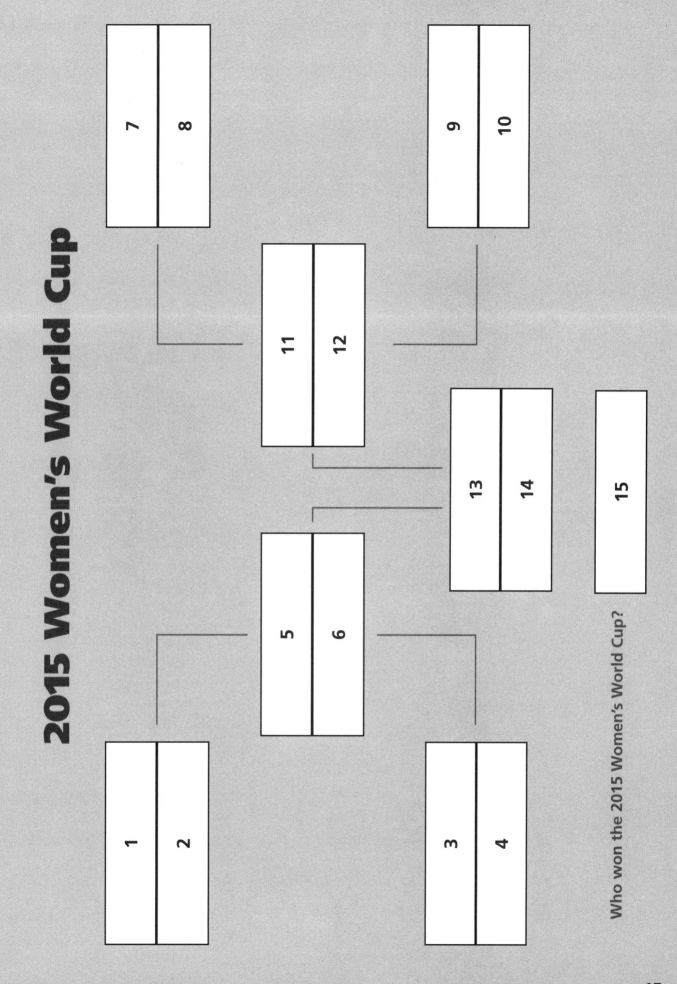

Who won the 2015 Women's World Cup?

Hiding in Plain Sight

Some animals can blend in with or look like what is around them. The colors or patterns on their bodies match their surroundings. This ability is called *camouflage*.

MAMMALS	BIRDS	REPTILES	INSECTS
Zebra	**Duck**	**Mata Mata Turtle**	**Katydid**
A zebra's stripes help it blend in with the tall grasses of the African savanna.	Most female ducks are brown. They blend in with the ground to help hide their nests.	This brown turtle lies at the bottom of muddy streams in South America.	This insect's body is green and shaped like a leaf.

  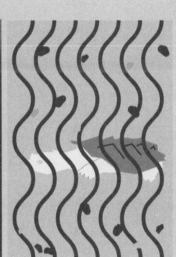 

Some animals use camouflage to hide from predators.

Some animals use camouflage to hunt for prey.

Polar Bear	**Eastern Screech Owl**	**Green Mamba**	**Praying Mantis**
The bear's white fur blends in with the Arctic landscape, allowing it to hunt for prey.	These birds blend in with the bark of trees. They sit quiet, still, and unseen, waiting for prey.	These green snakes live in the leafy, green treetops of Eastern Africa.	These insects can be green or brown. Their color and shape makes it difficult to tell them apart from leaves and twigs.

Think and Solve

Study the infographic. Answer the questions.

1. How are the animals in the top row different from the animals in the bottom row?

_____

2. Choose one example from the infographic. Explain how the animal uses camouflage.

_____

_____

_____

3. True or false? Female ducks use camouflage to help them hunt for insects.

_____

Show It

Read the description of each animal. Then, color the animals. Draw and color a habitat around each animal to show how it uses camouflage.

Crab spiders change colors to blend in. They hide on flowers to catch prey.

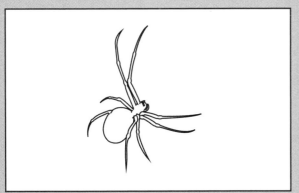

Stick insects look like twigs. They blend in with the plants and trees where they live.

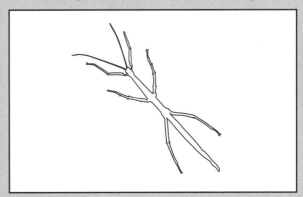

Arctic foxes have white coats. They blend in with the white snow so they can hunt.

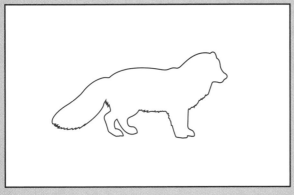

A **leaf-tailed gecko** looks like dead, dry leaves. It can easily hide from predators.

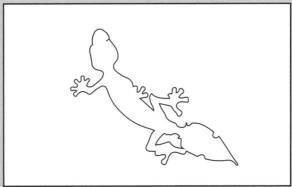

From Telephone to Smartphone

1876
First Phone
Alexander Graham Bell patents the telephone. Sound travels through electric wires from one phone to the other. This is how phones will work for the next 100 years until cell phones are invented.

1900
Candlestick Phone
The mouthpiece, or the part that you speak into, is at the top of the "candlestick." The receiver, or the part that you listen to, is on the end of a wire.

1977
Cordless Phone
The handset uses radio waves, not a cord, to connect to the main part of the phone. You cannot be too far away, or the handset will not work.

1984
Cell Phone
The first cell phones cost thousands of dollars and weighed almost 2 pounds!

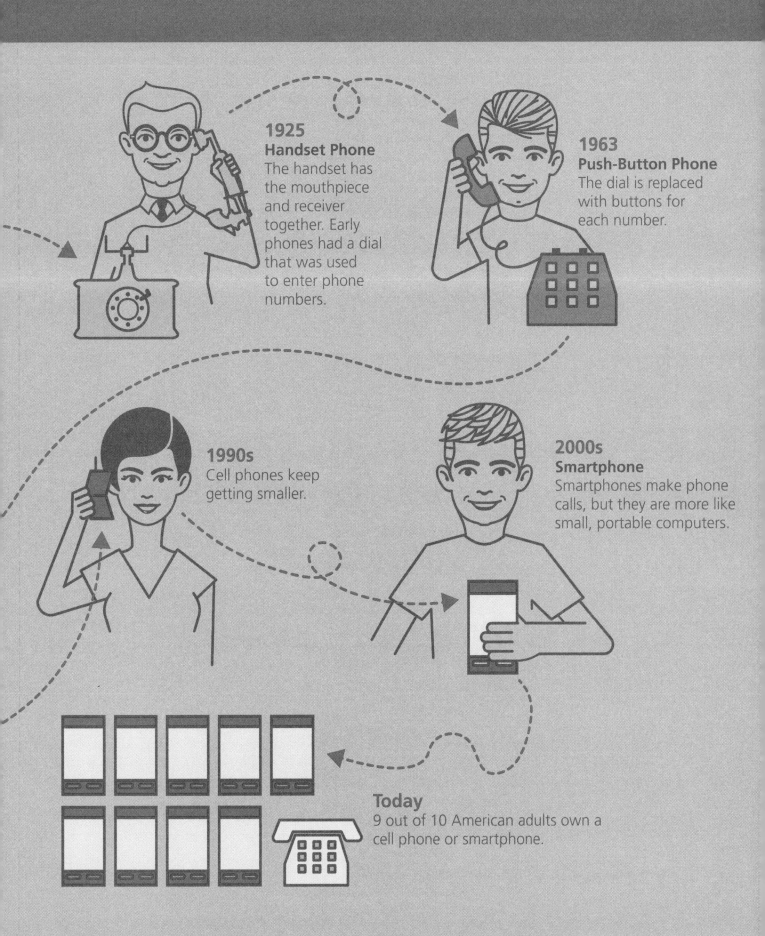

1925
Handset Phone
The handset has the mouthpiece and receiver together. Early phones had a dial that was used to enter phone numbers.

1963
Push-Button Phone
The dial is replaced with buttons for each number.

1990s
Cell phones keep getting smaller.

2000s
Smartphone
Smartphones make phone calls, but they are more like small, portable computers.

Today
9 out of 10 American adults own a cell phone or smartphone.

Think and Solve

Study the infographic. Answer the questions.

1. True or false? The telephone was invented more than 150 years ago.

_____

2. What is a phone's receiver used for?

_____

_____

3. How many American adults have cell phones today?
   A. 1 out of 9
   B. 1 out of 10
   C. 9 out of 10
   D. 10 out of 9

Make a Time Line

Read each description of a phone. Then, write the name of the phone and the date it was first used. Draw a line from the date to where it appears on the time line.

Name: _____ Alexander Graham Bell patents this phone. Date: _____	Name: _____ The receiver is on a wire, separate from the mouthpiece. Date: _____

1875

1900

Name: _____ The dial is replaced with buttons. Date: _____	Name: _____ This phone has a dial. Date: _____

1925

1950

Name: _____ This big, heavy phone is portable. Date: _____	Name: _____ Radio waves connect the handset to the main part of the phone. Date: _____

1975

2000

Draw and Write

How do you think phones will change in the future? What new features will they have? What new, amazing things will they do? Invent a phone from the future. Draw a picture of your phone in the box below. Then, write sentences to tell what it can do.

Phone of the Future

_____

_____

_____

_____

_____

_____

_____

_____

_____

_____

_____

_____

_____

_____

_____

_____

_____

Alligators vs. Crocodiles

Alligators

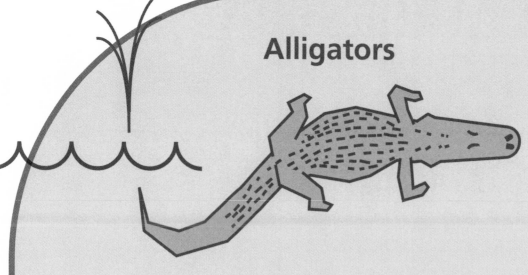

An alligator's jaw is rounded and shaped like a U.

Alligators are found in the United States, South America, and China.

Alligators live mostly in freshwater swamps and lakes.

An adult American alligator can grow up to 15 feet long and weigh up to 1,000 pounds.

When an alligator closes its mouth, all of its bottom teeth are hidden. You can still see its top teeth.

Both...

...are large reptiles.

...have webbed toes to help them swim.

...are carnivores, or meat-eaters, that live mostly in the water.

Southern Florida is the only place in the world where both crocodiles and alligators can be found.

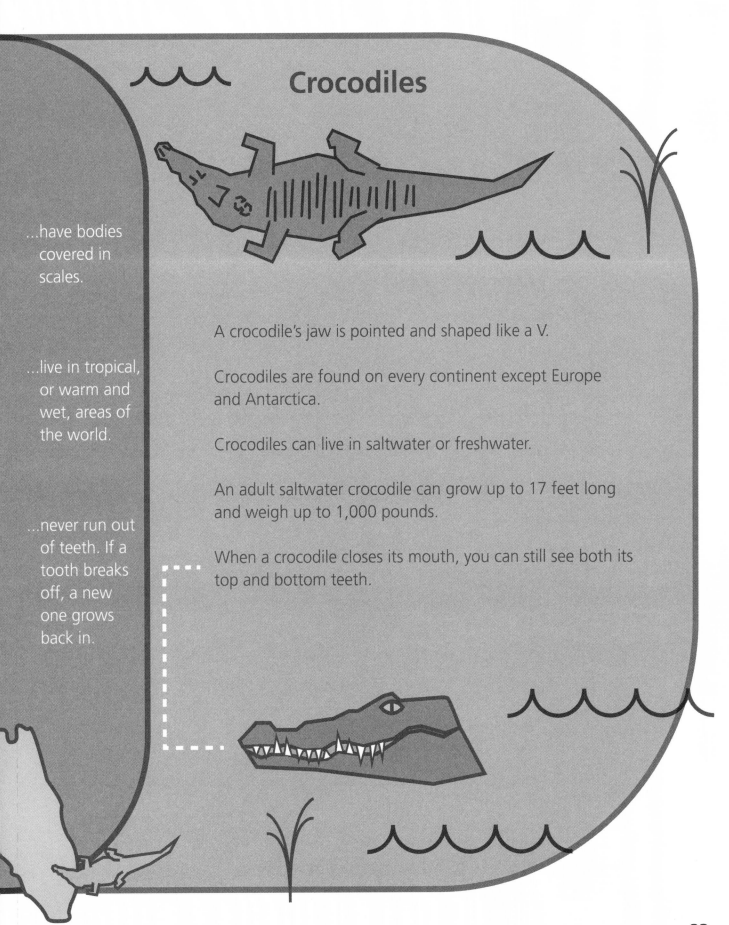

Crocodiles

...have bodies covered in scales.

...live in tropical, or warm and wet, areas of the world.

...never run out of teeth. If a tooth breaks off, a new one grows back in.

A crocodile's jaw is pointed and shaped like a V.

Crocodiles are found on every continent except Europe and Antarctica.

Crocodiles can live in saltwater or freshwater.

An adult saltwater crocodile can grow up to 17 feet long and weigh up to 1,000 pounds.

When a crocodile closes its mouth, you can still see both its top and bottom teeth.

Classify It

Read the facts about alligators and crocodiles. If the fact is true for alligators, write *A* on the line. If it is true for crocodiles, write *C*. If it is true for both, write *B*.

1. _____ I am a carnivore.

2. _____ I can grow to be 17 feet long.

3. _____ I can weigh up to 1,000 pounds.

4. _____ I have a U-shaped jaw.

5. _____ I am a reptile with scales that cover my body.

6. _____ When my mouth is closed, you can see only my top teeth.

7. _____ I can live in saltwater or freshwater.

8. _____ I can grow a new tooth if one breaks off.

9. _____ I have a V-shaped jaw.

10. _____ I have webbed toes.

Read About It: Seals vs. Sea Lions

SEALS AND SEA LIONS ARE BOTH PINNIPEDS. In Latin, *pinniped* means "fin-footed." Like walruses, these mammals spend time both in the water and on land.

Sea lions and seals are similar in some ways. For example, they both have flippers. They both eat fish. They also both have a thick layer of fat called *blubber* that keeps them warm.

Sea lions and seals also have differences. Sea lions have large flippers. This makes it easier for them to walk on land. Seals have smaller, stubby flippers, so they wriggle on land. They are better suited to life in the water.

Sea lions have earflaps. Seals have only holes for ears. Sea lions are noisy. They make loud barking sounds. Seals are quieter. They tend to make softer, grunting noises.

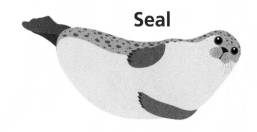
Seal

Sea Lion

The Visual Guide to Second Grade

Piece It Together

Cut out the facts. Decide whether each fact is true for seals, sea lions, or both. Glue or tape the facts in the correct places to make a Venn diagram on page 27.

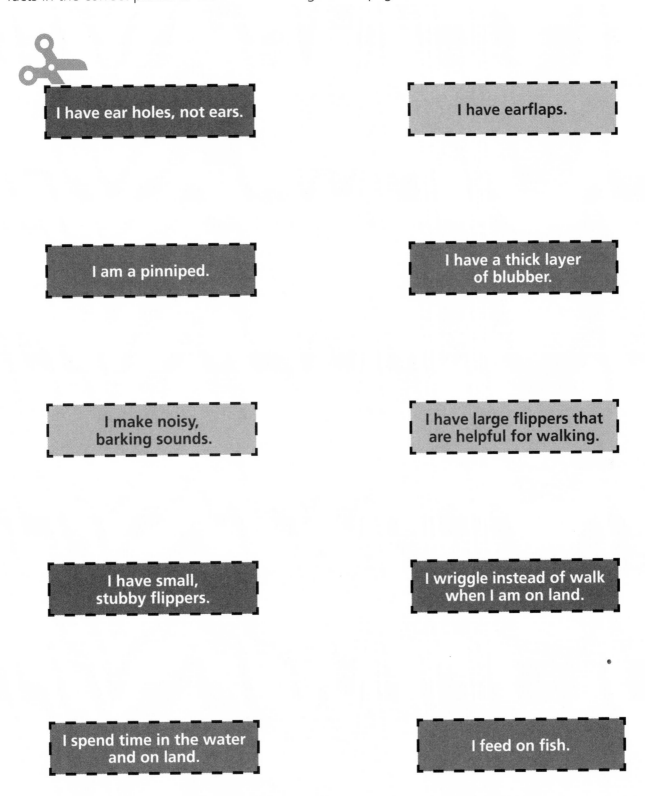

I have ear holes, not ears.

I have earflaps.

I am a pinniped.

I have a thick layer of blubber.

I make noisy, barking sounds.

I have large flippers that are helpful for walking.

I have small, stubby flippers.

I wriggle instead of walk when I am on land.

I spend time in the water and on land.

I feed on fish.

Venn Diagram

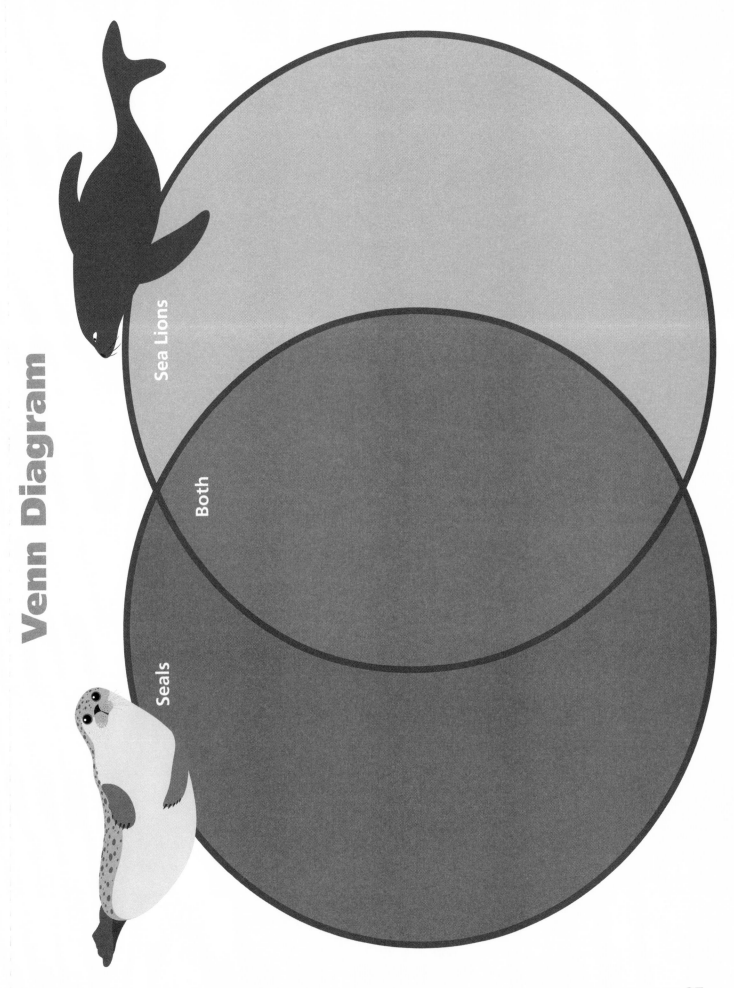

Sea Lions

Both

Seals

A Chilly Treat

Ice pops were first invented by a boy named Frank Epperson in 1905. He was only 11 years old! One day, he filled a glass with water. He used a wooden stick to stir in a powdered soda mix. He forgot the glass on the porch. At night, it froze. The next day, Frank ate the first ice pop. He called it the "Epperson icicle" or "Eppsicle." Later, he changed the name to Popsicle®.

An estimated 2 billion ice pops are sold each year!

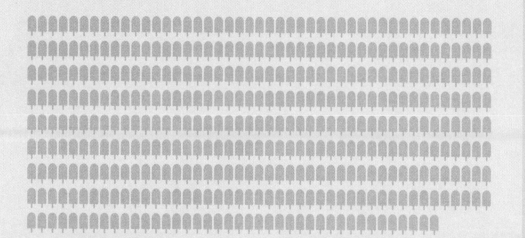

= 5 million ice pops

In 2009, Stephen Guman built a castle using 396,000 craft, or Popsicle® sticks and four gallons of white school glue. It was 12 feet tall and 16 feet deep. It was built with a drawbridge, an arch, and several towers.

Twin ice pops were first made during the Depression. That way, two kids could share one ice pop and save money.

Cherry is the most popular flavor of ice pop.

In England, ice pops are called "ice lollies." In Ireland, they are called "freeze pops."

Ice pops are one of the few foods we eat that changes states of matter. When you take one out of the freezer, it is a solid. On a hot day, it soon starts to melt. Now, part of it is a liquid!

Some flavors are a bit odd. Have you tried chocolate avocado? How about strawberry goat cheese or chili mango?

Think and Solve

Study the infographic. Answer the questions.

1. Ice pops were invented in _____.

    A. 1895

    B. 1905

    C. 1915

    D. 1925

2. True or false? In England, ice pops are called *ice lollies*.

_____

3. In the pictograph, each small ice pop is equal to _____ice pops sold in a year.

    A. 1 million

    B. 5 million

    C. 1 billion

    D. 2 billion

Make a Pictograph

Which flavors of ice pops do kids like best? Conduct a survey to find out. Ask at least 10 students what their favorite flavors are. Draw one ice pop for each answer. = one student

Flavor	Students Who Like the Flavor Best
Cherry	
Orange	
Lemon-Lime	
Grape	
Strawberry	
Other	

Snow Day!

States With Highest Single-Day Snowfalls

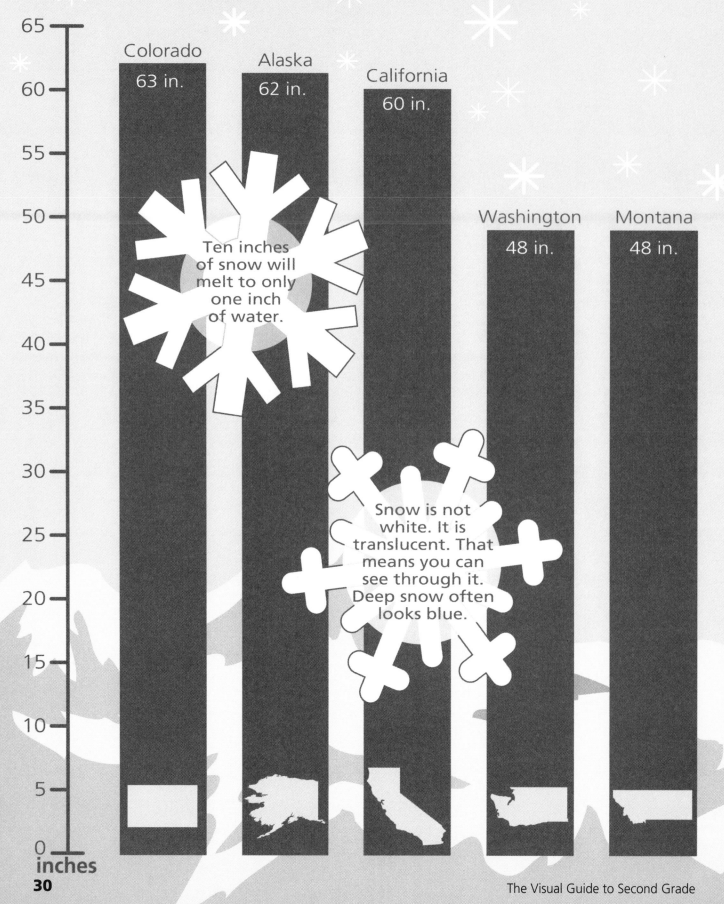

Colorado
63 in.

Alaska
62 in.

California
60 in.

Washington
48 in.

Montana
48 in.

Ten inches of snow will melt to only one inch of water.

Snow is not white. It is translucent. That means you can see through it. Deep snow often looks blue.

65
60
55
50
45
40
35
30
25
20
15
10
5
0

inches

How Does a Snowflake Form?

A snowflake is born when a water droplet sticks to a piece of dust and freezes. It forms an ice crystal. Ice crystals always have six sides. As the ice crystal falls to the ground, more droplets attach to it. They freeze too, and the ice crystal grows. But, it grows in a special way. Each side of the crystal grows in the same pattern.

South Dakota
47 in.

New York
45 in.

New Hampshire
41 in.

Pennsylvania
38 in.

Arizona
38 in.

Not all big snowstorms are blizzards. A blizzard lasts at least three hours. A blizzard also has strong winds. The winds blow the snow and make it hard to see. During a blizzard, you cannot see beyond $\frac{1}{4}$ of a mile, or 1,320 feet.

In the United States, at least 1 septillion ice crystals fall each winter. That's 1,000,000,000,000,000,000,000,000 or 24 zeros!

Try It Yourself

Follow the directions to make a beautiful paper snowflake.

1. Tear out page 33 from this book.

Cut out the square on that page.

2. Fold the square in half. The top left corner will fold down to the bottom right corner.

3. Fold the triangle in half. The top right corner will fold down to the bottom left corner.

4. Fold the triangle into thirds.

First, like this:  Then, like this:

Be sure the long sides are lined up evenly. This step may take some practice.

5. Cut a straight line across the bottom.

6. On the long sides and the bottom of the triangle, cut out shapes.

7. Unfold the paper to see your snowflake!

Think and Solve

Study the infographic. Answer the questions.

1. True or false? A blizzard happens when more than 12 inches of snow fall in an hour.

_____

2. All ice crystals have _____ sides.

A. 2

B. 4

C. 6

D. 8

3. What color is snow?

_____

4. If Wisconsin receives 46 inches of snow in a single day, where would it belong in the bar graph?

between _____ and _____

Do the Math

Solve the problems. Use the infographic to help you.

1. How much more snow did Colorado receive than New Hampshire?

_____inches

2. How many feet of snow did Montana receive? (Hint: 1 foot = 12 inches)

_____ feet

3. 60 inches of snow will melt to _____inches of water.

4. If Tennessee received half the amount of snow that Pennsylvania did, how much did Tennessee receive?

_____inches

5. How much snow did Colorado, Alaska, and California receive in total?

_____inches

The Global Orchestra

Mexico
marimba

- wooden bars of different lengths
- played by hitting the bars with mallets
- Marimbas first came from Africa. They were brought to Latin America by African slaves.

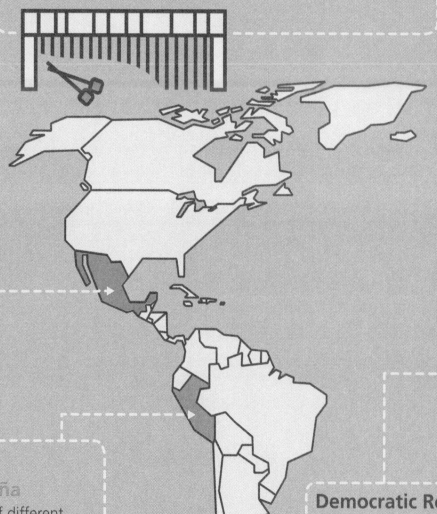

Peru
zampoña

- tubes of different lengths tied together
- played by blowing across the tops of the tubes
- The longer tubes make lower notes. The shorter tubes make higher notes.

Democratic Republic of the Congo
mbira

- wood or metal pieces of different lengths
- played by plucking the pieces with the thumbs
- The thin wood or metal pieces of the mbira are called *tongues*.

Middle East
oud
- stringed instrument with up to 12 strings
- played by strumming the strings with a pick
- Ouds have been around for thousands of years.

Russia
balalaika

- stringed instrument with 3 strings
- played by plucking the strings with the fingers
- The body of the balalaika is shaped like a triangle.

Japan
koto
- stringed instrument with 13 strings
- played by plucking the strings with the fingers
- A koto is about 6 feet long.

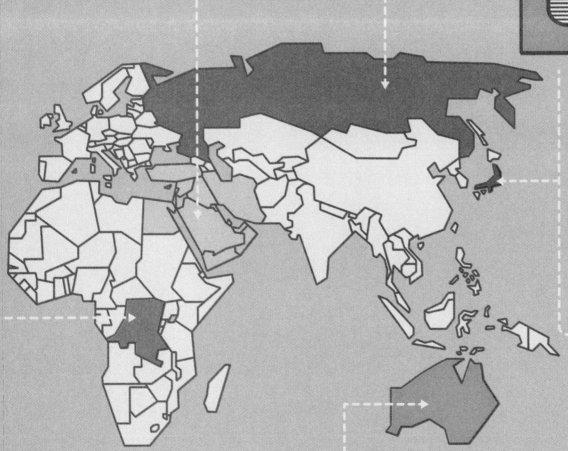

Australia
didgeridoo
- long, hollow tube made of wood, metal, or plastic
- played by blowing into the tube
- Some didgeridoos are more than 10 feet long!

Think and Solve

Study the infographic. Answer the questions.

1. The didgeridoo comes from _____.
   A. Mexico
   B. Australia
   C. Peru
   D. Japan

2. Choose two instruments. Tell one way they are alike and one way they are different.

   _____

   _____

3. True or false? When playing the zampoña, the shorter tubes make lower notes.

   _____

4. If you could learn to play one of these instruments, which one would you choose? Why?

   _____

   _____

Read About It: In the Orchestra

AN ORCHESTRA IS A GROUP of many musicians who play together. It is led by a conductor. The orchestra is divided into sections. Each section includes musicians who play similar instruments. There are four main sections. The first section is *strings*. String instruments, such as violins and cellos, make sound when long strings are plucked or played with a bow. The next section is *percussion*. Percussion instruments, such as drums and tambourines, are struck or shaken. The *woodwind* section contains instruments such as flutes that are played by blowing air through long, hollow tubes. The last section is *brass*. Brass instruments are made of metal. To play them, the musician blows air through a tube to make sound.

 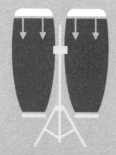 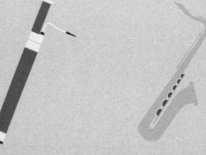

Classify It

Write the name of each instrument under the correct heading to show its section in the orchestra.

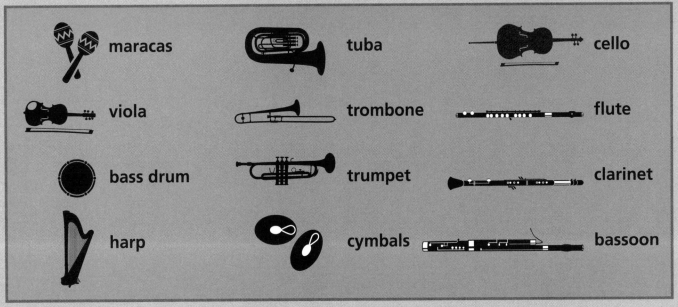

Percussion	Strings	Brass	Woodwinds
_____	_____	_____	_____
_____	_____	_____	_____
_____	_____	_____	_____

Try It Yourself

Even if you've never had a music lesson, you can learn to write music. There are seven notes you need to learn first. Each note has a letter name: A, B, C, D, E, F, and G. If you picture a piano keyboard, these same notes repeat. Have you ever heard someone sing, "Do, Re, Mi, Fa, So, La, Ti, Do"? If you have, you've heard a scale (or sequence) that includes each of the notes. The notes below show a scale beginning with middle-C. Try to sing, "Do, Re, Mi . . ." yourself to hear what each note sounds like.

Here are what the notes look like on a piano keyboard:

Now, try it yourself. Write a line of music in the space below.

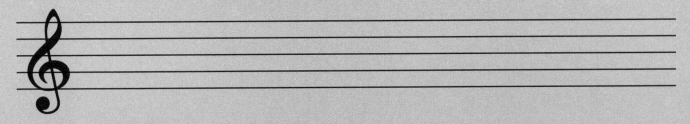

Too Sweet!

4 grams sugar = 1 tsp.

spaghetti sauce → 12 grams →

lemonade → 29 grams →

strawberry yogurt → 28 grams →

can of cola → 35 grams →

banana → 17 grams →

carrot → 4 grams →

peanut butter → 3 grams →

Young kids should have no more than 3–4 tsp. of added sugar a day (not including natural sugars in fruit, veggies, milk, etc.).

waffles and syrup → 37 grams →

*All measurements are per one serving. *Teaspoon measurements are approximate.

The Visual Guide to Second Grade

Think and Solve

Study the infographic. Answer the questions.

1. True or false? Three teaspoons of sugar equal 12 grams of sugar.

_____

2. Young kids should have no more than _____ teaspoons of added sugar each day.

How many grams of sugar are in four teaspoons? _____

3. How many teaspoons of sugar are in one serving of peanut butter and one banana?

    A. 5 teaspoons

    B. 7 teaspoons

    C. 12 teaspoons

    D. 15 teaspoons

4. How much more sugar does lemonade have than strawberry yogurt?

_____

Log It

Use the chart below to keep track of how many grams of sugar you eat in one day. List each food you eat and the number of grams of sugar it contains.

The amount of sugar in common foods is listed below. If the food you eat is not listed, check the infographic or the label on the package.

small apple = 11 g

clementine = 7 g

1 c strawberries = 7 g

baby carrots = $\frac{1}{2}$ g

cherry tomatoes ($\frac{1}{2}$ c) = 2 g

red potatoes ($\frac{1}{2}$ c) = 1 g

chicken breast = 0 g

beef hamburger = 0 g

beans ($\frac{1}{2}$ c) = 2 g

1 T honey = 17 g

granola bar = 12 g

bagel = 1 g

cornflakes = 2 g

vanilla ice cream = 28 g

milk (1 c) = 13 g

Key:

c = cup   g = gram T = tablespoon

Food	Grams of Sugar

Do you think you eat too much sugar? Why or why not?

_____

_____

Marvelous Monarchs

Have you ever seen a monarch butterfly? Most people know the monarch's orange and black coloring. Monarchs are common all over the US. Even so, spotting one is always special.

Life Cycle

Monarch caterpillars feed only on milkweed plants.

A monarch's bright colors are a warning to predators.

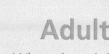

Adult

When the adult butterfly is ready, it comes out of the chrysalis. Its wings are damp at first. Once they dry, the butterfly can fly.

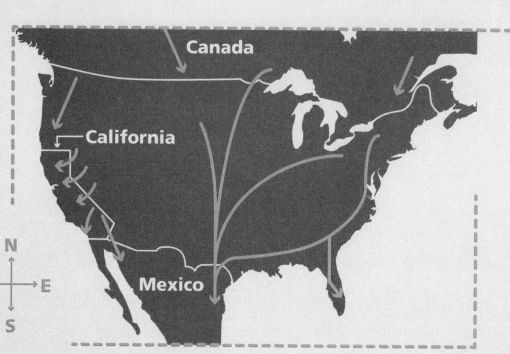

Canada

California

Mexico

N
W — E
S

Egg
Monarch eggs are usually laid on milkweed plants. They hatch about four days later.

Monarchs can travel from 50–100 miles a day.

Larva
The larvae, or caterpillars, eat their eggshells. Then, they feed on the milkweed plant where they were born.

Chrysalis
About two weeks later, the caterpillars make a case around themselves. It is called a *chrysalis*.

Monarchs have a life span of 6–8 weeks.

Monarch Migration
Every year, monarchs make an amazing journey. When it gets cold, they fly south. Most spend the winter in California or Mexico. The trip may be 3,000 miles long! Some parts of Mexico see up to a billion monarchs in the winter. No one is sure how the butterflies know where to go. As winter ends, they mate and then the males die. The females start the trip north again. Along the way, they lay their eggs. The cycle begins again.

The monarch wingspan measures about 4 inches.

4"

Think and Solve

Study the infographic. Answer the questions.

1. Write numbers 1–4 to put the stages of a monarch's life in order.

_____ chrysalis

_____ egg

_____ adult

_____ larva

2. Is a monarch's life span more or less than a month?

_____

3. Why don't male monarchs make the trip back north in the spring?

_____

4. True or false? Milkweed plants are poisonous to monarchs.

_____

Read About It:
Monarchs at Risk

MONARCH BUTTERFLIES ARE BEAUTIFUL. They are also fragile. Monarchs are in danger because of many changes taking place in the world today.

   Earth is getting warmer. It is also getting wetter. If monarchs get wet and then get very cold, they can freeze. They may also move north as temperatures warm up. This means they will have to migrate farther when it is time to travel south. We don't know yet if they will be able to do this.

   Another problem is that monarchs are losing their habitat. When forests are cut down, monarchs have fewer places to go. If milkweed plants disappear, monarch caterpillars have nothing to eat.

   To save the monarchs, we need to make sure that Earth stays a friendly place for butterflies to live.

Set Goals

Here are some ways people can help protect monarch butterflies. Set a goal. Check at least one thing you will do to help monarchs.

_____ Plant milkweed plants in your yard, school garden, or community garden.

_____ Write a letter to government leaders, asking for their help.

_____ Plant a wildflower garden.

_____ Write a letter to the Federal Highway Administration. Ask them to plant milkweed and flowers along highways instead of grass.

_____ Spread the word. Tell others about the trouble monarchs are in. Tell them how they can help.

_____ Ask your parents not to use pesticides in the yard. Pesticides can kill insects like butterflies.

_____ Observe monarchs and report your findings. Gathering information can help scientists!

Make a Plan

Choose one of the goals you checked. On the lines below, make a plan to reach your goal. Write each step in your plan. Then, do it!

1._____

_____

2._____

_____

3._____

_____

4._____

_____

Gifts From Ancient China

Gunpowder
c. AD 1000

Silk
c. 2700 BC

Printing
c. AD 800

The history of China begins more than 3,000 years ago. Since that time, Chinese culture has given the world many inventions and discoveries. Here are a few of Ancient China's most important inventions.

Paper Money
c. AD 750

Hang Glider
c. AD 600

c. = circa, or about

2000	1500	1000	500	0	500	1000	1500	2000
			BC		AD			

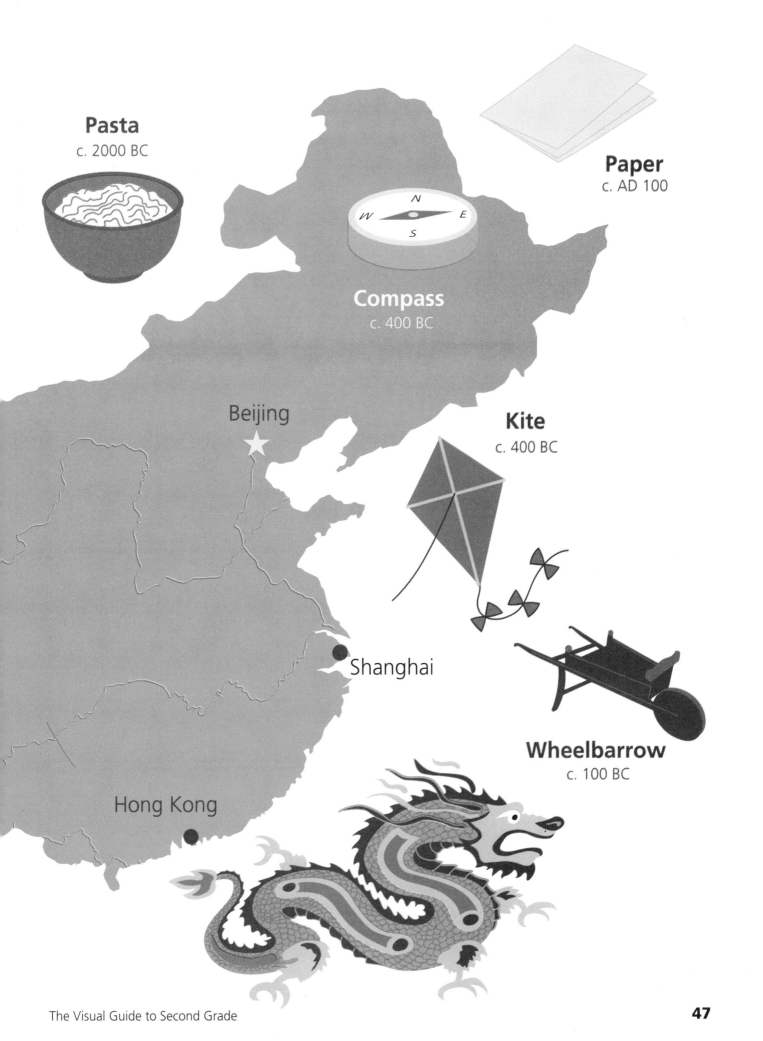

Pasta
c. 2000 BC

Paper
c. AD 100

Compass
c. 400 BC

N
W E
S

Kite
c. 400 BC

Beijing

Shanghai

Wheelbarrow
c. 100 BC

Hong Kong

Think and Solve
Study the infographic. Answer the questions.

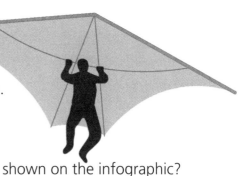

1. Silk was invented about _____ years before pasta.

2. Which is the newest invention shown on the infographic?
   A. gunpowder
   B. silk
   C. paper
   D. wheelbarrow

3. List the three cities shown on the map of China. Circle the name of the capital city.

_____

_____

_____

4. True or false? Paper was invented before kites.

_____

5. Which invention do you think was the most important? Why?

_____

_____

_____

6. True or false? The radio was invented in Ancient China.

_____

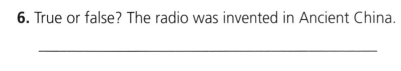

Write About It

Imagine if one of the inventions from Ancient China had never been made. How would your life be different? What would you use instead? Choose one invention from the infographic. Then, write about what life would be like today without it.

_____

_____

_____

_____

_____

_____

Try It Yourself

In the Chinese language, words are not written as groups of letters. Instead, each word is shown by its own set of lines called a *character*. The characters for three Chinese words are shown below. Practice writing the characters in the boxes.

纸   丝   風

paper   silk   wind

The Tip of the Iceberg

The tallest iceberg was about as tall as the Washington Monument!

168 m

Only $\frac{1}{10}$ of an iceberg can be seen above water. The rest is below the ocean's surface.

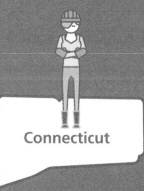

Connecticut

The largest iceberg was called B15. It was about 11,000 square km. That's almost as big as the state of Connecticut!

1 L water   1 L ice

1,000 g   920 g

Icebergs float because ice is less dense than liquid water. In other words, a certain amount of ice will weigh less than an equal amount of liquid water.

 < 15 m

Smaller icebergs are nicknamed "bergy bits" or "growlers." They may have cute names, but they are more dangerous than big icebergs. Bergy bits and growlers are harder to see in the water. There is a greater chance of a ship hitting one.

Icebergs form when chunks of freshwater ice break off of glaciers or ice sheets near Earth's poles. They fall into the ocean and drift with the ocean's current. This map shows where icebergs are found.

When icebergs reach warmer water, they break up and melt.

Think and Solve

Study the infographic. Answer the questions.

1. What fraction of an iceberg is under water?

_____

2. True or false? Icebergs are frozen chunks of salt water floating in the ocean.

_____

3. Why are small icebergs sometimes more dangerous than large ones?

_____

4. Icebergs are found _____.

    A. only at the North Pole

    B. only at the South Pole

    C. only in Iceberg Alley

    D. in the oceans near both poles

Try It Yourself

Icebergs float because ice is less dense (heavy) than liquid water. Try this experiment to prove it.

Materials:

- a clear cup
- food coloring
- baby oil
- vegetable oil
- an ice cube

Procedure:

1. Place a few of drops of food coloring in the cup.
2. Fill it halfway with vegetable oil. Fill it the rest of the way with baby oil.
3. Now, add the ice cube. It will float in the middle of the cup.
4. Be patient and watch. After a little while, the ice cube will start to melt.
5. The drops of water from the ice cube will sink to the bottom and mix with the food coloring.
6. The ice cube will keep floating. That's because ice is less dense than water!

First Pets

Americans love their pets. Presidents and their families are no different!
All kinds of animals have lived in the White House through the years.

138+

From Washington to Obama, almost every president has had at least one dog living in the White House as a pet. Many presidents had more. In fact, President Calvin Coolidge and his family had 12 dogs!

Abe Lincoln's son, Tad, kept a pet turkey named Jack. Jack was first sent to the White House to be part of Thanksgiving dinner!

Unusual White House Pets

badger

snake

donkey

bobcat

turkey

Snakes and a badger were just some of Teddy Roosevelt's many unusual pets.

President Coolidge had a donkey named Ebenezer and a bobcat named Smoky.

Many different birds have been pets in the White House: parrots, canaries, mockingbirds, a goose, and a macaw. President James Buchanan even had 2 bald eagles!

26+

One of the most popular White House pets of all time was Socks the cat. Socks lived with President Bill Clinton and his family.

14

--- Herbert Hoover kept a pet opossum.

President John Quincy Adams kept a pet alligator in the White House bathtub. One hundred years later, President Herbert Hoover's son brought two alligators to the White House as pets.

President Woodrow Wilson kept a flock of sheep on the White House lawn.

opossum

tiger cub

bear cub

alligator

sheep

President Martin Van Buren had a pair of tiger cubs.

President Thomas Jefferson had a pair of bear cubs.

The White House was crowded when President Theodore Roosevelt lived there. He and his wife had six children, but they also had a huge number of pets. Among their many pets were horses, dogs, birds, cats, snakes, a rabbit, a squirrel, guinea pigs, and a badger!

Think and Solve

Study the infographic. Answer the questions.

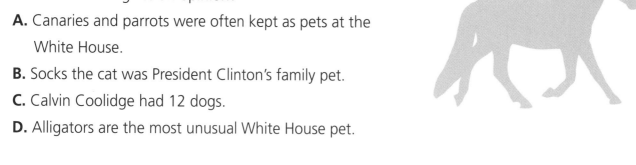

1. Which sentence gives an opinion?

   A. Canaries and parrots were often kept as pets at the White House.

   B. Socks the cat was President Clinton's family pet.

   C. Calvin Coolidge had 12 dogs.

   D. Alligators are the most unusual White House pet.

2. If you were president, what pets would you have? Why?

_____

3. True or false? Two presidents have kept alligators at the White House.

_____

4. Which animal is the most popular White House pet?

_____

5. _____ son rescued a turkey that was meant to be eaten for Thanksgiving dinner.

Do the Math

Solve the problems. Use the infographic to help you.

1. Write a number sentence to show the total number of bear and tiger cubs Jefferson and Van Buren had.

_____

2. Have there been more dogs or birds in the White House? Which number sentence shows the correct answer?

   A. 26 > 14

   B. 138 < 26

   C. 138 > 26

   D. 26 < 14

Collect Data

Ask 20 people you know what pets they have. Record their answers in the chart. Make an X in the box to show each pet a person owns. (For example, if your aunt has three cats, make three Xs in the box next to *Cat*.) Add the Xs to find a total for each type of pet.

What Pets Do People Own?

ANIMAL		TOTAL
Cat		
Dog		
Fish		
Rabbit		
Guinea Pig/ Hamster		
Snake		
Other		

Make a Bar Graph

Now, make a bar graph to show the data you collected. For each animal, use the number from the TOTAL column in the chart above. Draw a bar above the animal name that reaches as high as the number on the left side that is closest to your total. Make each bar a different color.

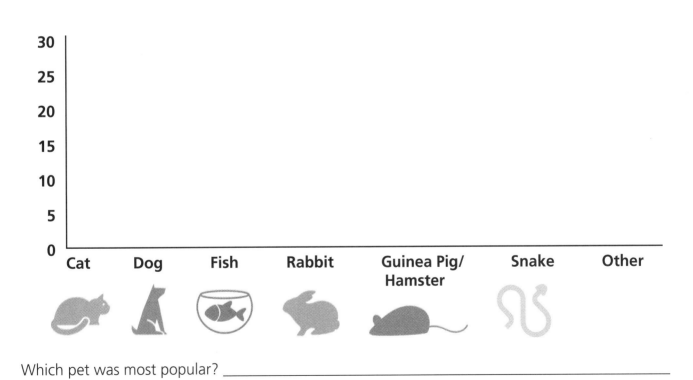

Which pet was most popular? _____

Which pet was least popular? _____

Pop! Pop! Pop!

Popcorn is one of the most POP-ular snacks in America. Each year, about 16 billion quarts of popcorn are eaten in the United States!

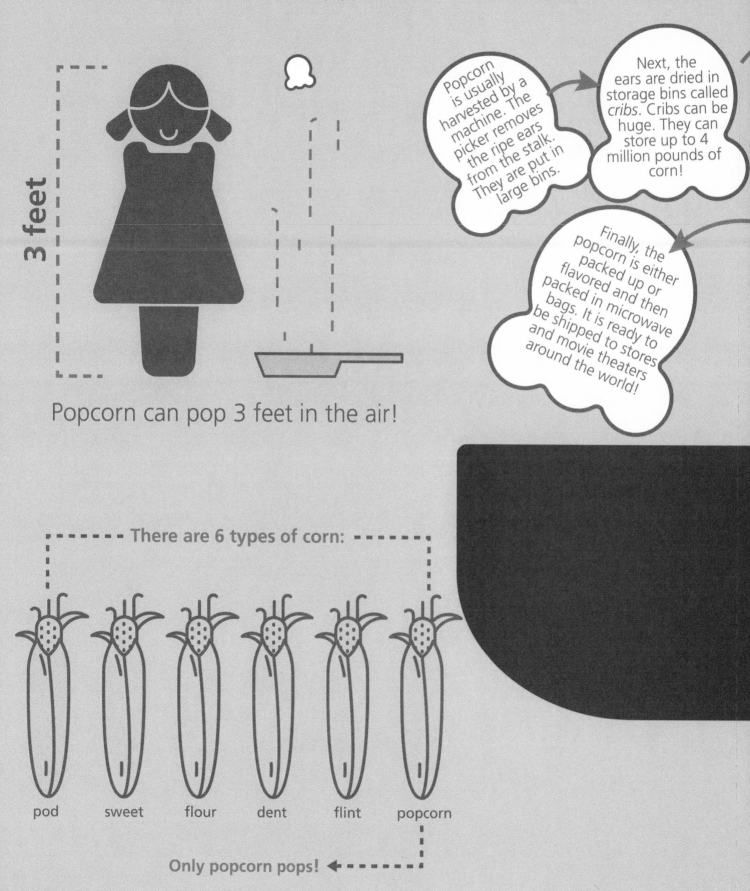

3 feet

Popcorn can pop 3 feet in the air!

Popcorn is usually harvested by a machine. The picker removes the ripe ears from the stalk. They are put in large bins.

Next, the ears are dried in storage bins called *cribs*. Cribs can be huge. They can store up to 4 million pounds of corn!

Finally, the popcorn is either packed up or flavored and then packed in microwave bags. It is ready to be shipped to stores and movie theaters around the world!

There are 6 types of corn:

pod sweet flour dent flint popcorn

Only popcorn pops! ←

POP

Once the ears are dry, a machine called a scalper strips the kernels off.

The kernels are sent to the fanning mill. Dust is blown off them. Workers check that the kernels are good quality.

Now, the kernels are cleaned and polished. Any bad kernels—or ones that are too big or too small—are separated out.

Why does popcorn pop?
Inside each unpopped kernel is a small drop of water. The drop is surrounded by starch. As the kernel heats up, the water gets heated and the starch melts. When water reaches about 212°F, it turns into steam. Steam needs more space than liquid water. The steam pushes against the sides of the kernel. When the kernel reaches about 347°F, the steam pressure is too strong. The kernel bursts open. The starch spills out and puffs up as it cools. The starch turns into a solid again. That's the puffy (and tasty!) part of popcorn we love! A popped piece of popcorn is about 40 times bigger than the unpopped kernel.

In the United States, most popcorn is grown in the Midwest. Nebraska, Iowa, Missouri, Illinois, Indiana, Ohio, and Kentucky grow the most.

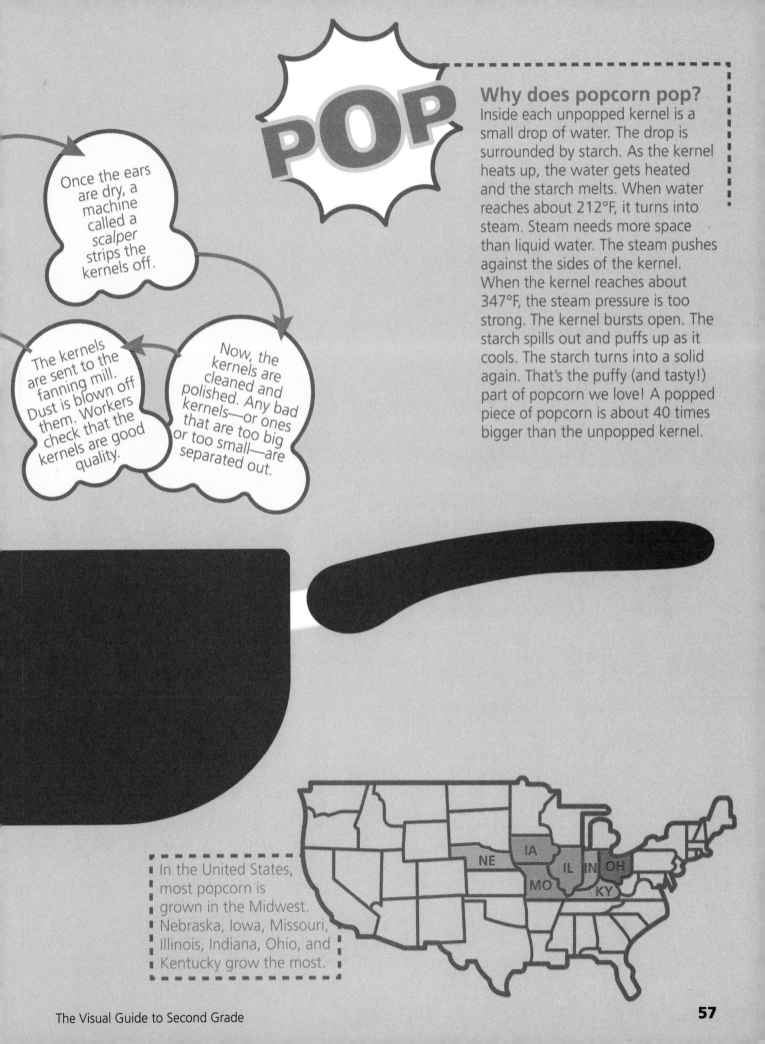

NE IA
IL IN OH
MO KY

POP

1. What happens to popcorn kernels at the fanning mill?

_____

2. True or false? All of the top popcorn-growing states are in the same area of the United States.

_____

3. If a kernel of popcorn has no water in it, what do you think will happen when it is heated?

_____

4. About how many quarts of popcorn do Americans eat in a year?

   A. 16,000,000

   B. 16,000,000,000

   C. 16,000

   D. 1,600

5. Popcorn pops when the kernel reaches

about _____degrees.

6. How high can a popcorn kernel pop into the air?

   A. 3 inches

   B. 12 inches

   C. 24 inches

   D. 36 inches

Try It Yourself

If you heat 100 kernels of popcorn, how many of them will pop? With an adult's help, follow the directions to find out.

1. Make a prediction.

Number of kernels that will pop: _____

Number of kernels that will not pop: _____

2. Count out 100 unpopped popcorn kernels.

3. Pour enough oil into a small pot to cover the bottom. Heat the oil and add one kernel.

4. As soon as the kernel pops, add the other 99 kernels. Gently shake the pot so all the kernels are covered in oil. Put a lid on the pot.

5. As soon as the popping stops, take the pot off the heat.

6. Let the popcorn cool. Pour the popcorn onto a plate or tray. Count the number of unpopped kernels. How close was your prediction? Fill in the blanks to show your results.

Number of kernels that did not pop: _____

100 − _____ = _____
        number that   number that
        did not pop   did pop

Make a Pie Chart

Make a pie chart to show how many kernels popped and how many kernels did not pop. Use the key to color the pie chart. Each section of the chart equals five kernels. (You may need to round your results up or down in order to make the chart.)

Key:

▢ = popped kernels

▢ = unpopped kernels

Why do you think the unpopped kernels did not pop?

_____

_____

Let the Games Begin

London 2012 Summer Olympics

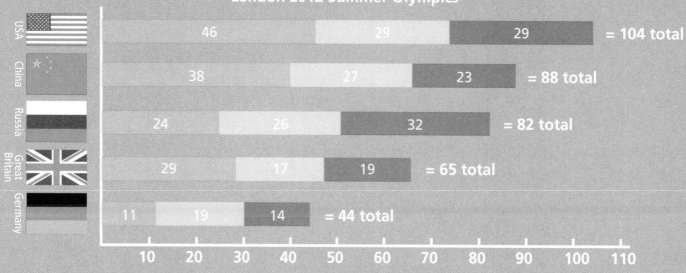

USA	46	29	29	= 104 total
China	38	27	23	= 88 total
Russia	24	26	32	= 82 total
Great Britain	29	17	19	= 65 total
Germany	11	19	14	= 44 total

10 20 30 40 50 60 70 80 90 100 110

Norway has won the most medals at the Winter Games.

Until 1994, the Olympics were every 4 years. After that, they changed to every 2 years—switching between summer and winter.

The Olympic motto is in Latin. In English it means, "Faster, Higher, Stronger."

Africa, South America, and Antarctica are the only continents that have never hosted the Olympics.

Sochi 2014 Winter Olympics

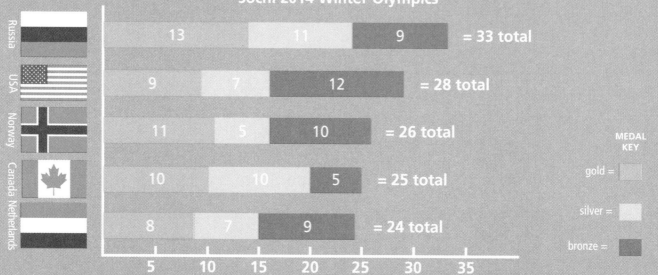

Russia	13	11	9	= 33 total
USA	9	7	12	= 28 total
Norway	11	5	10	= 26 total
Canada	10	10	5	= 25 total
Netherlands	8	7	9	= 24 total

5 10 15 20 25 30 35

MEDAL KEY

gold =

silver =

bronze =

Piece It Together

Cut out the labels that show Olympic events. Some of the events are part of the Winter Olympics. Some of them are part of the Summer Olympics. Glue or tape the labels under the correct headings on page 63.

volleyball

figure skating

snowboarding

soccer

luge

fencing

swimming

hockey

gymnastics

skiing

bobsled

equestrian

basketball

speed skating

ski jumping

cycling

Olympic Events

Winter Olympics

Summer Olympics

Earth's Tropical Rain Forests

Where are the tropical rain forests?

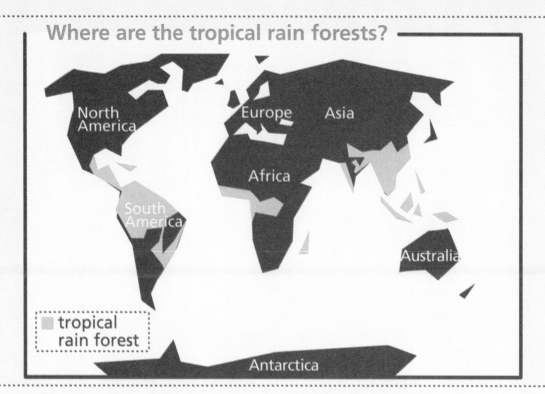

North America

Europe

Asia

Africa

South America

Australia

■ tropical rain forest

Antarctica

What would you find in one square mile of a tropical rain forest?

400
different kinds of flowering plants

140
different kinds of trees

100
different kinds of butterflies

40
different kinds of birds

Humans have cut down about $\frac{3}{5}$ of Earth's rain forests.

Tropical rain forests are warm, wet, wooded places. They are filled with trees, plants, and animals.

A tropical rain forest can get about 150 inches of rain in a year. The United States gets about 30 inches per year.

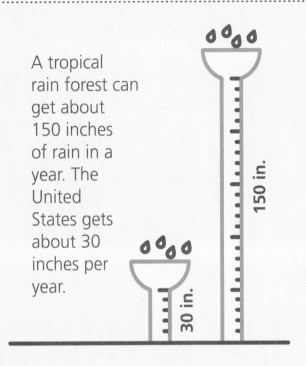

150 in.

30 in.

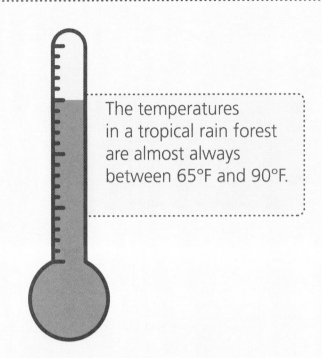

The temperatures in a tropical rain forest are almost always between 65°F and 90°F.

Where do plants and animals live? Half of Earth's plants and animals live in rain forests!

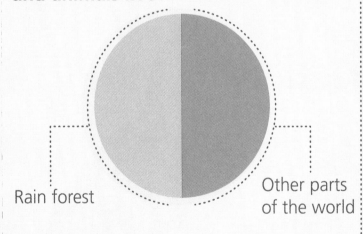

Rain forest

Other parts of the world

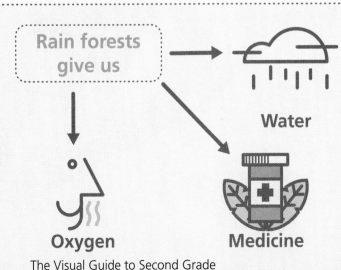

Rain forests give us

Water

Oxygen

Medicine

Did you know?
Not all rain forests are warm! Rain forests can be found in cooler parts of the world, too. They are called *temperate rain forests.*

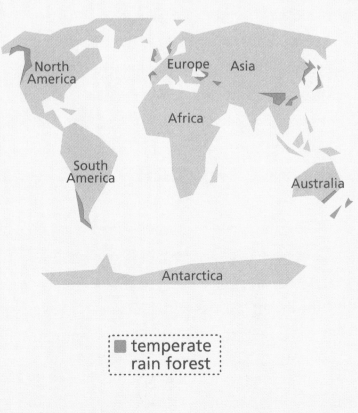

North America

Europe   Asia

Africa

South America

Australia

Antarctica

■ temperate rain forest

Study the infographic. Answer the questions.

1. True or false? A temperate rain forest is hotter than a tropical rain forest.

_____

2. About how much rain does a tropical rain forest get in a year?

_____

3. Humans have chopped down more than half of Earth's tropical rain forests. About_____
of the rain forests are left.

   A. $\frac{4}{5}$

   B. $\frac{3}{5}$

   C. $\frac{2}{5}$

   D. $\frac{1}{5}$

4. True or false? The temperatures in tropical rain forests don't usually drop below 65°F.

_____

Read About It: Layers of Life

RAIN FORESTS ARE FILLED WITH LIFE. Different
animals live in each of four layers of a rain forest.
These layers go from the giant treetops all the
way down to the forest floor. The *emergent
layer* is at the top, towering up to 200 feet above
the ground. This layer gets the most sun. Only the tallest
trees reach this level. Birds, monkeys, and butterflies are found there.

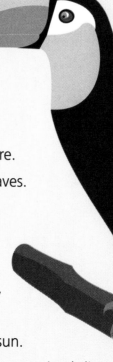

   The next layer is the *canopy.* This layer is thick and dense with leaves.
Many animals, such as toucans, sloths, lizards, snakes, and tree
frogs, live there.

   Below the canopy is the *understory.* It does not get much sun.
Plants have larger leaves in this layer. There are many vines. Insects,
as well as jaguars, leopards, and frogs live there.

   The lowest layer is the *forest floor.* It is very damp and gets little sun.
Things rot quickly on this layer. Few plants grow. The largest rain forest animals live
there and in the understory.

Piece It Together

Cut out the pictures of animals that live in the rain forest. Glue or tape them in the correct rain forest layers on page 69. The colors of the labels will help you know which layer to place them in.

emerald tree boa

harpy eagle

spider monkey

giant armadillo

centipede

morpho butterfly

toucan

peccary (wild pig)

beetle

cockroach

bat

salamander

jaguar

pygmy anteater

howler monkey

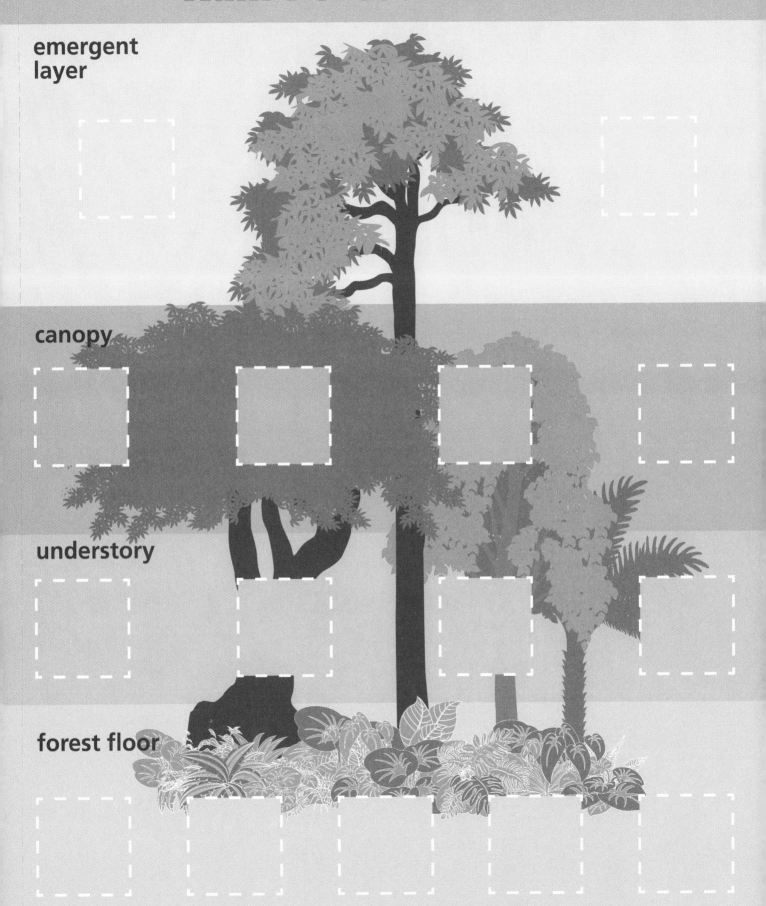

emergent layer

canopy

understory

forest floor

Fighting Fires

Face Shield
protects the face and
eyes from heat, smoke,
and debris

Reflective Stripes
help firefighters spot
each other through
the smoke

Gloves
thick and padded so firefighters
can touch hot things

Axe
to break down doors,
windows, walls, or roofs

Boots
thick rubber with
steel toes

Helmet
protects firefighters
from heat and
falling objects

Air Mask

Air Hose
allows the firefighter
to breathe safely while
looking for victims and
putting out the fire

Turnout Pants & Coat
waterproof and
heatproof fabric helps
keep firefighters safe

Air Tank

Wow! A firefighter's gear tips
the scale at about 75 pounds!
That's a lot of extra weight
to carry.

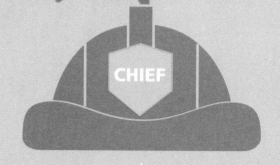

Gear costs a lot. A helmet costs about
$200. A turnout coat costs about $800!

Think and Solve

Study the infographic. Answer the questions.

1. Why does a firefighter carry an axe?

_____

2. True or false? A firefighter's gear weighs more than 100 pounds.

_____

3. Read each sentence. Write *F* if the sentence tells a fact. Write *O* if it tells an opinion.

_____ A firefighter's hat costs about $200.

_____ The most important piece of equipment is the air tank.

_____ Hiking boots are more comfortable than steel-toe boots.

_____ Thick, padded gloves protect a firefighter's hands.

4. Write the names of two other pieces of firefighting equipment not shown in the infographic.

_____ and _____

5. What is special about the fabric used to make a turnout coat and pants?
   A. It is very light.
   B. It is waterproof and heatproof.
   C. It is made of rubber.
   D. It glows in the dark.

Classify It

These words and phrases relate to firefighting. Write *N* beside each noun (naming word).
Write *V* beside each verb (action word). Write *A* beside each adjective (describing word).

_____ hot	_____ expensive	_____ smoke	_____ debris
_____ fire	_____ to break	_____ to breathe	_____ victims
_____ to fight	_____ roof	_____ to spray	_____ mask
_____ safe	_____ reflective	_____ to protect	_____ thick
_____ padded	_____ waterproof	_____ heavy	_____ to help

Let's Go to the Park!

Mount Rainier
Established: 03-02-1899
Size: 235,625 acres
Visitors in 2014:
  1,264,259
Highlight: glaciers

Glacier
Established: 05-11-1910
Size: 1,013,572 acres
Visitors in 2014:
  2,338,528
Highlight: glaciers

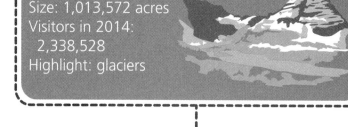

Crater Lake
Established: 05-22-1902
Size: 183,224 acres
Visitors in 2014: 535,508
Highlight: Crater Lake,
deepest lake in the
United States

Yosemite

Established: 10-01-1890
Size: 761,266 acres
Visitors in 2014:
  3,882,642
Highlight: Yosemite Falls,
the tallest waterfall in
North America

Yellowstone
Established: 03-01-1872
Size: 2,219,790 acres
Visitors in 2014:
  3,513,484
Highlight: Old Faithful
and other geysers

Rocky Mountain
Established: 01-26-1915
Size: 265,828 acres
Visitors in 2014: 3,434,751
Highlight: Bear Lake

The United States of America has many special natural places. In the late 1800s, an important idea was born: Natural places could be protected by turning them into parks. Today, there are 59 National Parks in the United States.

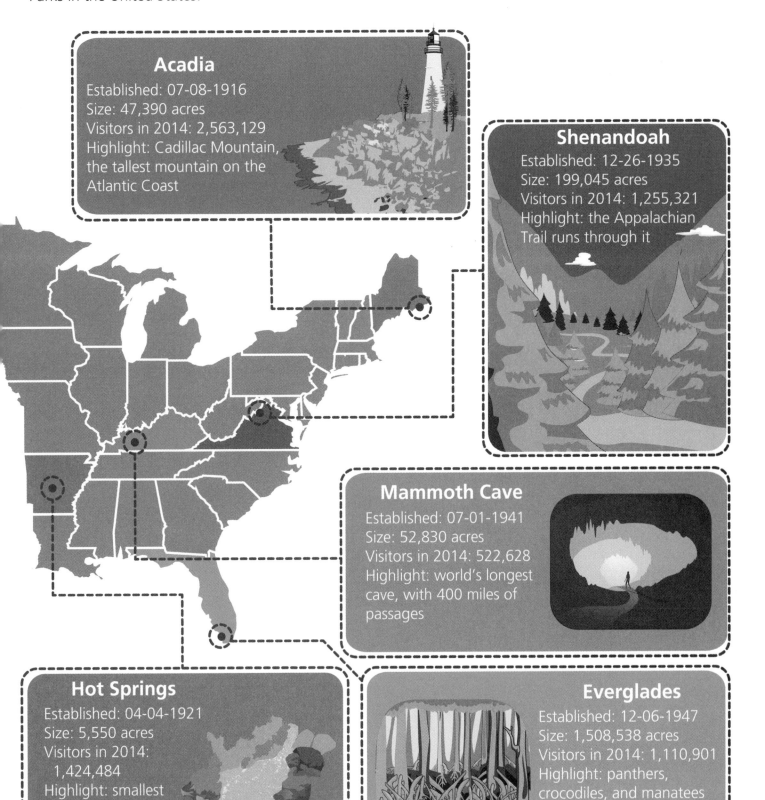

Acadia
Established: 07-08-1916
Size: 47,390 acres
Visitors in 2014: 2,563,129
Highlight: Cadillac Mountain, the tallest mountain on the Atlantic Coast

Shenandoah
Established: 12-26-1935
Size: 199,045 acres
Visitors in 2014: 1,255,321
Highlight: the Appalachian Trail runs through it

Mammoth Cave
Established: 07-01-1941
Size: 52,830 acres
Visitors in 2014: 522,628
Highlight: world's longest cave, with 400 miles of passages

Hot Springs
Established: 04-04-1921
Size: 5,550 acres
Visitors in 2014:
   1,424,484
Highlight: smallest National Park and the only one in a city

Everglades
Established: 12-06-1947
Size: 1,508,538 acres
Visitors in 2014: 1,110,901
Highlight: panthers, crocodiles, and manatees live here

Think and Solve

Study the infographic. Answer the questions.

1. Where is the tallest waterfall in North America?

_____

2. True or false? The tallest mountain in the United States is Cadillac Mountain in
Acadia National Park.

_____

3. Crater Lake is the_____ lake in the United States.
   A. biggest
   B. oldest
   C. deepest
   D. coldest

4. Which park is the largest National Park shown in the infographic?

_____

Make a Time Line

Make a time line to show when National Parks were established (founded). Write the names
of the parks in the spaces on the time line. Use the infographic to help you.

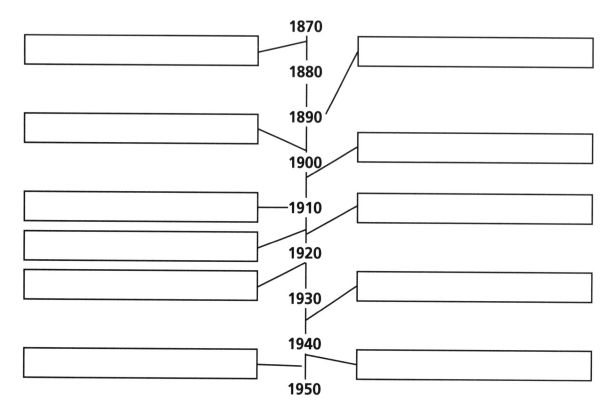

Make a Chart

Complete the chart. List the five parks from the infographic that had the most visitors in 2014.

National Parks with the Most Visitors, 2014

Rank	Park Name	Number of Visitors
1st		
2nd		
3rd		
4th		
5th		

Schedule It

Imagine you have one week to visit three National Parks. Which ones will you choose to see? How many days will you stay at each park? Remember, you will need to drive from one park to the next. Choose parks that are near each other. Fill in the calendar to plan your week.

Sunday	Monday	Tuesday	Wednesday	Thursday	Friday	Saturday

Which park would you most like to visit? Why?

_____

_____

_____

_____

Listen Up!

What is sound? Sound is waves moving through the air. You use your ears to sense the movement.

Pitch

Pitch is how high or low a sound is. Pitch is measured in hertz, or Hz. Hertz is how many waves go by in one second.

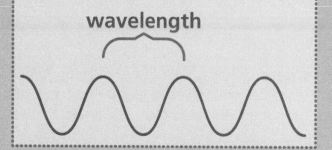

wavelength

Low pitch sounds have longer wavelengths.

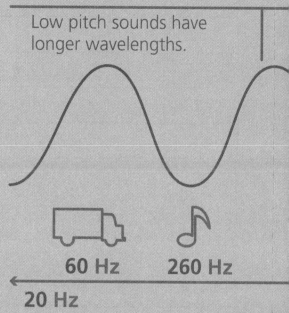

60 Hz   260 Hz

20 Hz

Loudness

How loud or soft a sound is depends on the size of the wave. Loudness is measured in decibels, or dB.

size

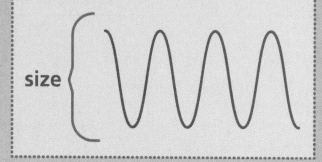

Quieter sounds have smaller waves.

30 dB   60 dB

Sound waves go deep into your ear and hit your eardrum. They cause your eardrum to vibrate. Your brain reads the vibrations and tells you what you are hearing.

Drop a pebble in water. You will see waves spread out from where the pebble hit. Sound works in a similar way. Hit a bell, and it will vibrate. As the bell vibrates, it pushes on the air around it. It makes waves in the air. The waves move through the air and into your ear. That's sound!

Humans can hear sounds between 20 Hz and 20,000 Hz.

High pitch sounds have shorter wavelengths.

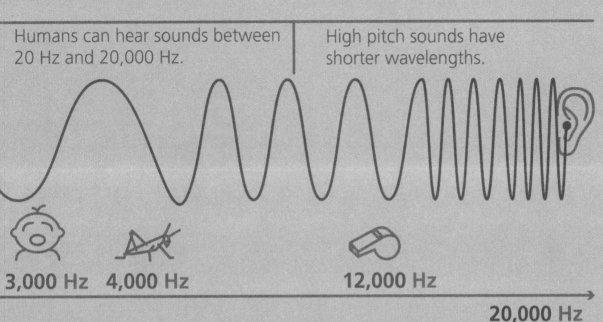

3,000 Hz   4,000 Hz   12,000 Hz

20,000 Hz

Sounds above 85 dB can damage your hearing. Sounds above 120 dB can cause pain.

Louder sounds have taller waves.

100 dB   110 dB   120 dB   140 dB

In 1883, the volcano Krakatoa exploded. The sound could be heard almost 3,000 miles away. At about 180 dB, it may be the loudest sound ever heard by humans.

Think and Solve
Study the infographic. Answer the questions.

1. True or false? A sound that is 4,000 Hz is always louder than a sound that is 60 Hz.

_____

2. Sounds above _____dB can cause pain.

   A. 60

   B. 85

   C. 100

   D. 120

3. A truck goes by. The sound it makes has a pitch of 50 Hz. What does this information tell you?

   A. The truck made a high sound.

   B. The truck made a low sound.

   C. The truck is loud.

   D. The truck is quiet.

4. A radio is turned up to 75 dB. Describe where you would place the radio in the infographic.

_____

_____

5. A dog whistle makes a sound at 30,000 Hz. What does this tell you about dogs?

_____

6. Smaller waves go together with (quieter, louder) sounds.

_____

7. Explain how hearing works.

_____

_____

Collect Data
Perform a hearing test. Follow the directions below. Record the results.

What you need:
- a large, quiet room with a hard floor
- a paper towel
- a tape measure
- three people to test
- a piece of paper and a pencil

What you do:

1. Squish the paper towel into a tight ball.

2. Have one person sit facing the wall.

3. Use the tape measure to measure one foot from the person's back. Stand at that spot.

4. Tell the person facing the wall to listen closely. Say, "When you hear the paper towel hit the floor, raise your hand."

5. Hold the paper towel ball six inches above the floor. Drop it.

6. The person facing the wall will raise his or her hand.

7. Hold the paper towel ball six inches above the floor again. This time, drop it two feet away from the person's back.

8. The person facing the wall will raise his or her hand.

9. Keep dropping the paper towel ball from the same height. Each time, move one foot farther away. Stop when the person no longer hears the paper towel hit the floor.

10. Record the farthest distance the person could hear the paper towel. Repeat the test with two more people.

Make a Bar Graph
Make a graph to show the results of your hearing test. Write the name of each person you tested on a line. Then, for each person, color a square above each distance from which he or she could hear the paper towel drop.

Hearing Test Results

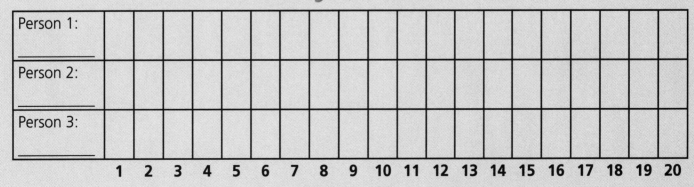

Distance in Feet

Two American Greats: George and Abe

 VS.

| George Washington b. 1732–d. 1799 | Abraham Lincoln b. 1809–d. 1865 |

He was born in Virginia.  He was born in Kentucky.

He married Martha Dandridge in 1759. He was a stepfather to her two children. He never had children of his own.   He married Mary Todd in 1842. They had four children together.

General Washington led the American troops to victory in the Revolutionary War.  Before he became president, he gave many powerful speeches against slavery. They made him famous.

He was the 1st president of the United States (1789–1797). He served two terms.  He was the 16th president of the United States (1861–1865). He was president during the Civil War. He was elected again in 1864. In April 1865, he was shot and killed.

He is buried in Mount Vernon, Virginia.  He is buried in his hometown of Springfield, Illinois.

The Washington Monument is a famous landmark in Washington, DC.  The Lincoln Memorial is a famous landmark in Washington, DC.

Washington appears on the $1 bill and the 25¢ coin (quarter).   Lincoln appears on the $5 bill and the 1¢ coin (penny).

The Visual Guide to Second Grade

Piece It Together

Now, compare two different US presidents. Cut out the facts. Decide whether each fact is true about President Theodore Roosevelt, President John F. Kennedy, or both. Glue or tape the facts in the correct places to make a Venn diagram on page 83.

Theodore Roosevelt was the 26th president.

Kennedy and Roosevelt both went to Harvard.

Kennedy was a Democrat.

John F. Kennedy was the 35th president.

Roosevelt became president after President McKinley was shot.

Kennedy and Roosevelt both fought in wars.

When elected, Kennedy and Roosevelt were both the country's youngest president.

Kennedy was assassinated while in office.

Roosevelt loved nature and worked to protect the nation's forests.

Kennedy created the Peace Corps to help people in struggling nations.

Roosevelt was a Republican.

Kennedy and Roosevelt were both born into wealthy families.

Venn Diagram

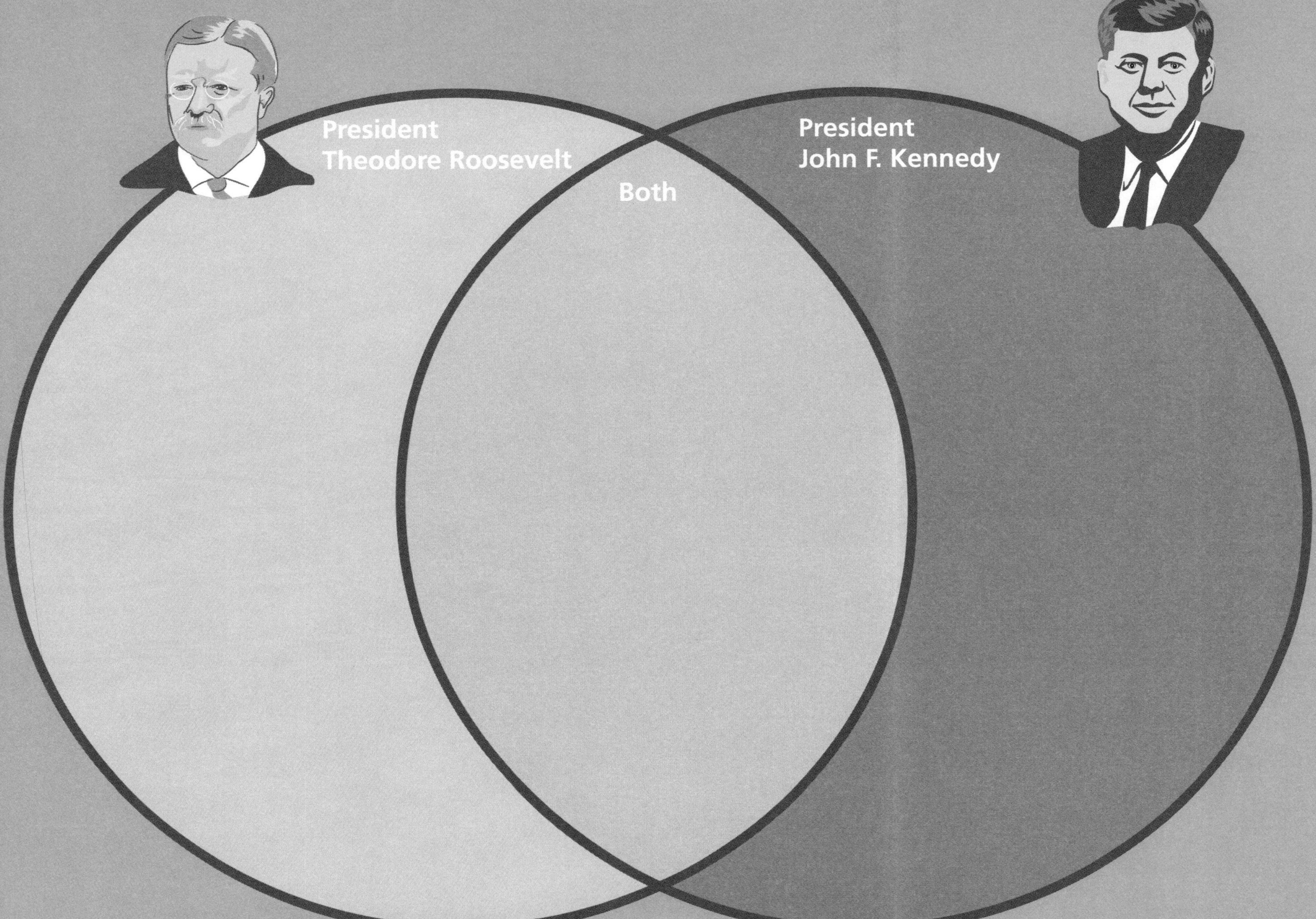

President
John F. Kennedy

Both

President
Theodore Roosevelt

Mountains of Fire

Magma is molten, or melted, rock deep inside Earth. When magma flows up to Earth's surface, it forms a volcano. Magma that reaches Earth's surface is called *lava*. Some volcanoes ooze lava slowly and steadily. But some do not. Instead, the way to Earth's surface is blocked. Pressure builds up inside the volcano. When the pressure is too much, the volcano explodes! It spews lava and ash across the land. This map shows some of Earth's most famous volcanic eruptions.

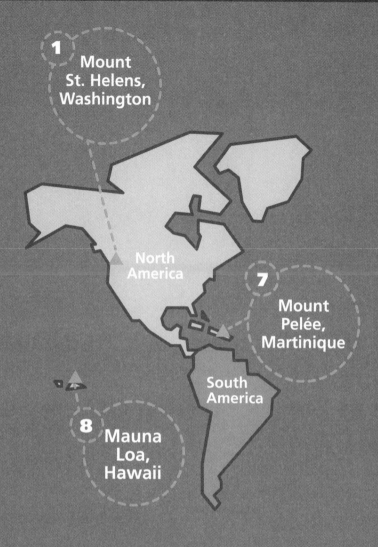

1 Mount St. Helens, Washington

North America

7 Mount Pelée, Martinique

South America

8 Mauna Loa, Hawaii

1. Mt. St. Helens shot out ash and stone at speeds of 300 mph. The black ash covered parts of three states!

Mt. St. Helens

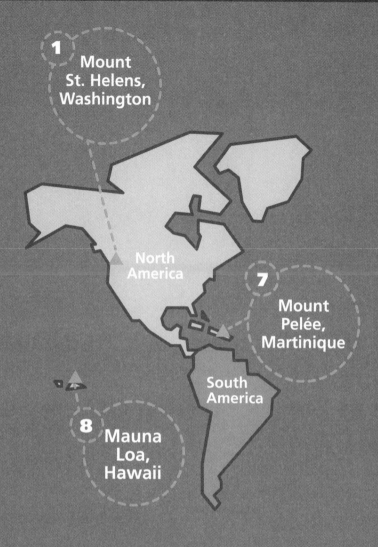

2. Eyjafjallajökull is not the biggest or fiercest of volcanoes. But, in 2010, it had a large eruption. It shot ash miles into the air.

Eyjafjallajökull

5. Mt. Tambora's eruption in 1815 was one of the biggest volcanic eruptions ever recorded. It caused giant waves called *tsunamis* (soo na' meez).

Mt. Tambora

6. Krakatoa's eruption in 1883 was many times stronger than an atom bomb! It could be heard thousands of miles away.

Krakatoa

2 Eyjafjallajökull, Iceland

3 Mount Vesuvius, Italy

4 Mount Pinatubo, Philippines

5 Mount Tambora, Indonesia

6 Krakatoa, Indonesia

Asia

Europe

Africa

Australia

When pressure builds up, the volcano erupts and spews lava and ash.

Volcanoes form when magma from inside Earth makes its way to the surface.

3. Mt. Vesuvius is one of the world's most famous volcanoes. Almost 2,000 years ago, there was a huge eruption. It completely covered the city of Pompeii.

Mt. Vesuvius

4. Mt. Pinatubo blew in 1991. It was the first eruption in about 600 years. It sent so much ash into the air, temperatures cooled by 1°F for the next two years!

Mt. Pinatubo

7. Mt. Pelée erupted above the city of St. Pierre in 1902. It traveled at a speed of over 100 mph and reached the town in less than a minute!

Mt. Pelée

8. Mauna Loa is one of the world largest volcanoes—it is almost 14,000 feet tall. It is also one of the most active. It has erupted 33 times since 1843.

Mauna Loa

Think and Solve

Study the infographic. Answer the questions.

1. True or false? *Magma* and *lava* both mean "molten rock."

_____

2. Which volcano is the most active?

   A. Mauna Loa

   B. Mt. Vesuvius

   C. Mt. St. Helens

   D. Krakatoa

3. How many volcanoes shown in the infographic are in the United States?

_____

4. What is a tsunami?

   A. an earthquake caused by a volcano

   B. a volcano that oozes lava steadily

   C. a giant wave

   D. another name for magma

Classify It

Use the infographic. Write the name of each volcano under the name of the continent where it is found. Hint: You will not use every line.

Africa	Asia	North America	South America	Australia	Europe
_____	_____	_____	_____	_____	_____
_____	_____	_____	_____	_____	_____
_____	_____	_____	_____	_____	_____

Match It

Draw a line to match each fact with the name of the volcano it describes.

erupted above St. Pierre

almost 14,000 feet tall

one of the biggest eruptions ever recorded

erupted in 2010

its eruption was many times stronger than an atom bomb

destroyed Pompeii 2,000 years ago

erupted in 1991 and affected temperatures for two years

shot ash and stone at speeds of 300 miles per hour

Mt. Tambora

Mt. Vesuvius

Mt. Pinatubo

Mauna Loa

Krakatoa

Mt. Pelée

Mt. St. Helens

Eyjafjallajökull

Try It Yourself

Make your own volcano! With an adult's help, follow the steps below. Be sure to make your volcano in a place that can get messy.

What you need:
- clay
- a small container, such as a yogurt cup
- tablespoon
- baking soda
- dish soap
- red and yellow food coloring
- vinegar

baking soda

What you do:

1. Use the clay to form a mountain with the container in the middle. Be sure the container is open at the top.

dish soap

2. Pour **two tablespoons of baking soda** into the container.

food coloring   4 drops red   4 drops yellow

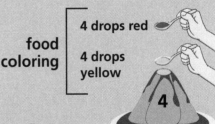

3. Pour **one tablespoon of dish soap** into the container.

4. Add **four drops of red food coloring and four drops of yellow food coloring**.

5. Add **two tablespoons of vinegar** and watch out!

Lady Liberty

TORCH

The torch is a symbol of enlightenment (a state of knowledge and understanding). Today's torch is covered in 24K gold. It reflects the sun during the day. It is lit up at night.

The people of France gave the Statue of Liberty to America in 1886. It was a gift of friendship. The statue was a symbol of democracy and freedom. A sculptor named Frédéric-Auguste Bartholdi built the statue in sections. It was shipped to the US in 350 pieces. It took four months to put it together!

Why is she green?

The Statue of Liberty is made of copper, like pennies are. When it was first built, it was a brownish color. It took 30 years for the copper to weather and turn green.

Winds of 50 mph make the statue sway about 3 inches. The torch sways about 6 inches.

CROWN

There are seven spikes on the crown. Some believe these stand for the seven seas and seven continents. There are 25 windows in the crown.

TABLET

On the tablet, the date of America's independence is carved: July 4, 1776. The date and year are written in Roman numerals.

JULY IV MDCCLXXVI

CHAINS

Broken chains around the statue's feet are a symbol of American independence.

305 ft. 1 in. (from the ground to the tip of the flame)

The statue's face may resemble the sculptor's mother.

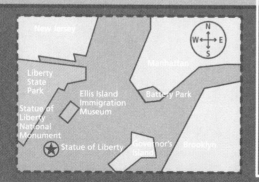

Read About It: Ellis Island

ELLIS ISLAND IS A SMALL ISLAND in New York. In 1892, it opened as an immigration station. People came from other countries by boat. At Ellis Island, they learned if they could stay in America. They had to show that they were healthy. They answered many questions. Could they read and write? Did they have family in the US? Did they have any money? Did they speak English? Those who passed the test were allowed into the country. Others had to wait. Some were sent back home. Today, about four out of every ten Americans have a relative who passed through Ellis Island!

The first immigrants came through Ellis Island in **1892**. There were about 450,000 that year. For the next ten years, the numbers were steady: **1893** (350,000), **1894** (200,000), **1895** (200,000), **1896** (250,000), **1897** (200,000), **1898** (200,000), **1899** (250,000), **1900** (350,000), **1901** (400,000), **1902** (500,000). The numbers grew even higher in the years right before World War I.

Think and Solve
Study the infographic and the passage above. Answer the questions.

1. True or false? The Statue of Liberty was a gift to America from the people of England.

_____

2. Brooklyn is _____ of the Statue of Liberty.
   A. north
   B. east
   C. south
   D. west

3. Because the statue is made of _____, it turned from brown to green.

4. How did people arrive at Ellis Island?

_____

5. True or false? More people wanted to come to the US right before World War I began.

_____

Make a Line Graph

Use the information you read about Ellis Island to make a line graph. Find each year along the bottom of the graph. Above it, follow the squares going up until you reach the number on the left side that matches the number of immigrants who came through Ellis Island during that year. Draw a dot at that spot. Connect all the dots to form a line.

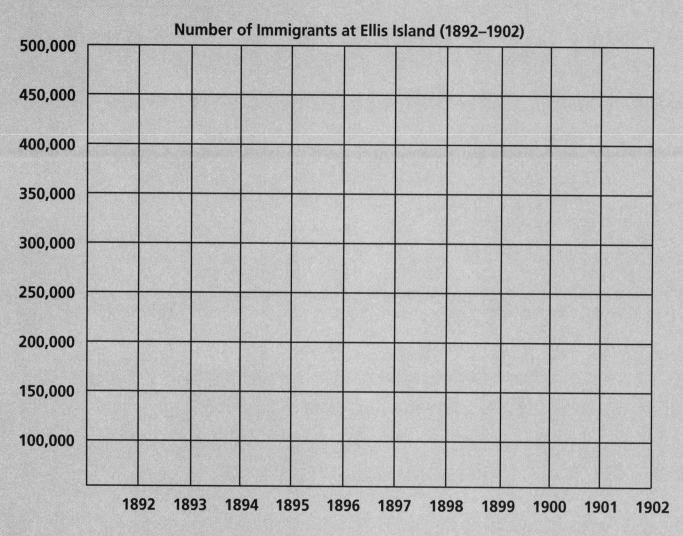

Number of Immigrants at Ellis Island (1892–1902)

Does the line between 1892 and 1894 go up or down? _____

Did the number of immigrants from 1892 to 1894 go up or down? _____

Does the line between 1898 and 1902 go up or down? _____

Did the number of immigrants between 1898 and 1902 go up or down? _____

Map It

Where in the world is your family from? Talk to your parents or other relatives. Find out what part of the world your family comes from. Color those areas on the world map. On the lines below the map, write about your family's history. Tell when members of your family moved to new places and how they got there.

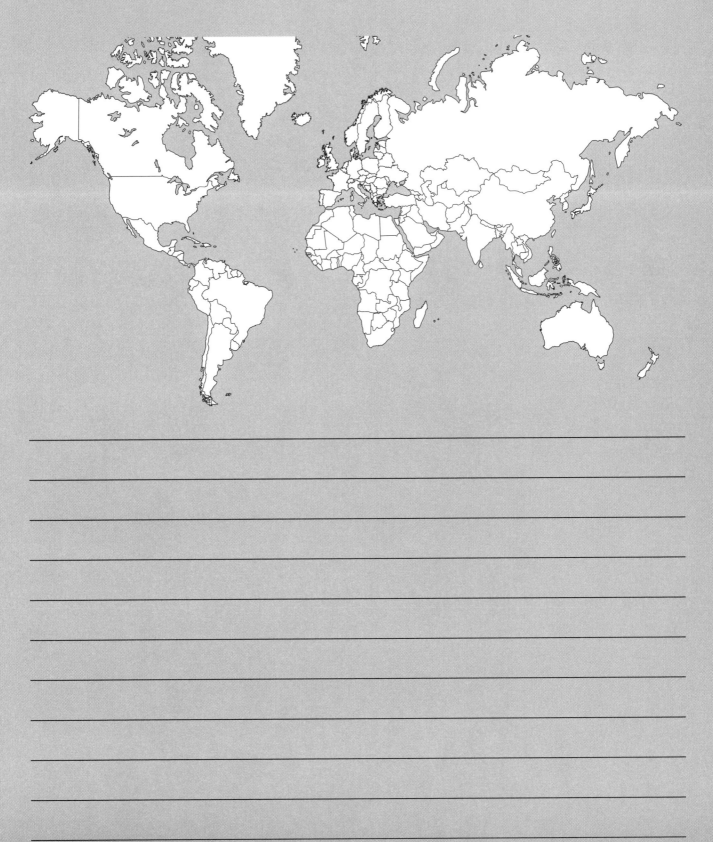

_____

_____

_____

_____

_____

_____

_____

_____

_____

_____

_____

From Bean to Bar

Most people love chocolate. We eat it plain, as well as in candy bars, cakes, cookies, ice cream, and hot drinks. Do you know where this tasty sweet comes from?

Workers HARVEST pods from cacao trees, which grow in tropical places, like Central and South America. They open up the pods and scoop out the beans.

Next, the beans and pulp from the pods are FERMENTED for about a week. Bacteria works on the beans and causes them to change color and develop flavor. After they are DRIED, they are shipped out.

The beans are then ROASTED by chocolate makers. This helps to further develop the flavor.

After roasting, the beans are CRACKED and WINNOWED, which means that large fans blow away the shells. The nibs or "meat" of the beans are left behind.

How Many Pounds of Chocolate Do Americans Eat Each Year?

= 1 pound

The nibs are GROUND into a paste called *cocoa liquor*. Then, they are CONCHED, or mixed, with sugar, milk, and other flavorings.

Finally, the chocolate is TEMPERED. This is a process of heating and cooling the chocolate carefully so that certain types of crystals form.

The chocolate is now ready to be MOLDED, or poured into molds and shaped. Before you know it, the chocolate will be on the shelf of a store, waiting for you to purchase it!

What Are the Most Popular Holidays for Chocolate Sales in the US?

1. **Christmas ($409 million)**

2. **Halloween ($406 million)**

3. **Easter ($323 million)**

4. **Valentine's Day ($245 million)**

Think and Solve

Study the infographic. Answer the questions.

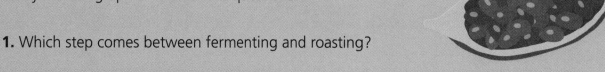

1. Which step comes between fermenting and roasting?

_____

2. True or false? Tempering the chocolate means heating and cooling it.

_____

3. Number the following steps in the order in which they occur.

_____ The nibs are ground into paste.

_____ The chocolate is poured into molds to shape it.

_____ The roasted beans are cracked.

4. How much more chocolate is sold at Christmas than at Halloween?

_____

Log It

Keep track of how many ounces of chocolate you eat in the next two weeks.

Ounces of Chocolate Eaten per Day

	Sunday	Monday	Tuesday	Wednesday	Thursday	Friday	Saturday
Week 1							
Week 2							

Make a Pictograph

Now, make a pictograph to show how much chocolate you ate in two weeks.

Use the key.   = 1 ounce of chocolate

Try It Yourself

Read the list of things to make with chocolate. Make a check mark beside one thing that you can explain how to make.

☐ chocolate milk

☐ hot chocolate

☐ chocolate sundae

☐ s'more

☐ trail mix

☐ chocolate milkshake

☐ yogurt with chocolate chips

☐ chocolate-covered pretzel

Make a Process Chart

Think about the chocolate treat you chose above. Write it on the line below. Then, draw and write in the spaces to explain each step you need to follow to make the treat.

How to Make _____

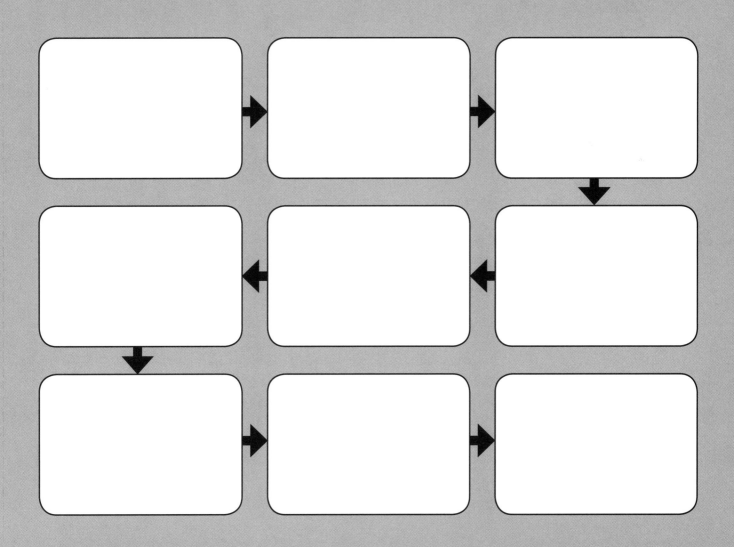

Get Your Head in the Clouds

▶ Cumulonimbus
Cumulonimbus clouds are thunderheads. They are very tall. Their tops are sometimes as high as 50,000 feet. They are filled with energy and can cause lightning, make hail, or create a tornado.

Cirrocumulus

Cirrocumulus clouds are made of ice. When the sky is covered with cirrocumulus clouds, it is sometimes called a "mackerel sky." A mackerel is type of fish, and the clouds look like fish scales.

Stratus clouds are what you see on a gray, sunless day. They are flat and cover the sky. High stratus clouds are called altostratus. When they are near the ground and causing rain, they are called nimbostratus clouds.

Altostratus

Cumulus

Stratus

Cumulus clouds are big, puffy, white clouds. On hot days, they can turn into cumulonimbus clouds.

I hope those thunderheads don't move this way!

Gaze up at the sky. What do you see? The clouds above us are not all alike. Depending on the weather and the altitude (height), different types of clouds appear.

Cirrus

Cirrus clouds are thin and wispy. They are made of ice. They do not make rain. Cirrus clouds are nicknamed "mare's tails" because they look like a horse's tail.

Altocumulus clouds are long lines of puffy clouds.

Altocumulus

Those clouds look like fish scales!

I knew that was a nimbostratus cloud!

Nimbostratus

Thousands of Feet

30

27

24

21

18

15

12

9

6

3

Think and Solve

Study the infographic. Answer the questions.

1. Explain one difference between nimbostratus clouds and altostratus clouds.

_____

2. A sky with _____clouds is sometimes called a *mackerel sky.*

3. Which clouds are usually higher in the sky—cirrus clouds or altocumulus clouds?

_____

4. Which type of clouds can turn into thunderheads?
   A. stratus
   B. cumulus
   C. cirrus
   D. cumulonimbus

Match It

Draw lines to match the clouds with their descriptions.

stratus   long lines of puffy clouds

cumulonimbus   called "mare's tails" and
                                                     do not make rain

cirrus   can cause lightning, hail, or a tornado

cumulus   clouds on a gray, sunless day

altocumulus   puffy white clouds that can turn
                                                     into cumulonimbus clouds

Explore Your World

Once each day, go outside and watch the clouds in the sky. Draw what you see. Below each drawing, write the names of the types of clouds you saw.

Day One	Day Two

Cloud Types: _____

_____

Cloud Types: _____

_____

Day Three	Day Four

Cloud Types: _____

_____

Cloud Types: _____

_____

Author! Author!

Who are your favorite authors? Are they the same authors you liked when you were younger? Some of the best-loved books have been around for many years. How many of the books shown below have you read?

Beverly Cleary
Born: April 12, 1916
- She loves to write books that make children laugh.
- won the Newbery Medal in 1984

The Mouse and the Motorcycle · *Henry and Ribsy* · *Ramona Quimby, Age 8* · *Otis Spofford* · *Ellen Tebbits* · *Strider*

Number of Children's Books Written*

Roald Dahl
Born: September 13, 1916
- He wrote all of his stories with a pencil and yellow paper.
- More than half of his books have been made into movies.

The BFG · *Charlie and the Chocolate Factory* · *Fantastic Mr. Fox* · *James and the Giant Peach* · *Matilda* · *Revolting Rhymes*

Number of Children's Books Written

Dr. Seuss
Born: March 2, 1904
- full name is Theodor Seuss Geisel
- not really a doctor
- *The Cat in the Hat* uses 225 words and *Green Eggs and Ham* uses exactly 50.

The Cat in the Hat · *Green Eggs and Ham* · *Horton Hears a Who* · *How the Grinch Stole Christmas* · *If I Ran the Circus* · *The Lorax*

Number of Children's Books Written

Cynthia Rylant
Born: June 6, 1954
- Her first book only took one hour to complete.
- won the Newbery Medal in 1993

Cobble Street Cousins · *Henry and Mudge* · *The High Rise Private Eyes* · *Lighthouse Family* · *Mr. Putter and Tabby* · *Poppleton*

Number of Children's Books Written*

 = 4 books

*as of 2015

Write About It

Cut out the bookmarks. Fill in the titles and authors of books you have read. Then, write a short review for each one. Tell what you liked about each book. Share your completed bookmarks with friends.

Title:

_____
_____

Author:

_____
_____

I thought this book was:

_____
_____
_____
_____
_____
_____
_____
_____
_____
_____
_____
_____
_____

Title:

_____
_____

Author:

_____
_____

I thought this book was:

_____
_____
_____
_____
_____
_____
_____
_____
_____
_____
_____
_____
_____

Title:

_____
_____

Author:

_____
_____

I thought this book was:

_____
_____
_____
_____
_____
_____
_____
_____
_____
_____
_____
_____
_____

Title:

_____
_____

Author:

_____
_____

I thought this book was:

_____
_____
_____
_____
_____
_____
_____
_____
_____
_____
_____
_____
_____

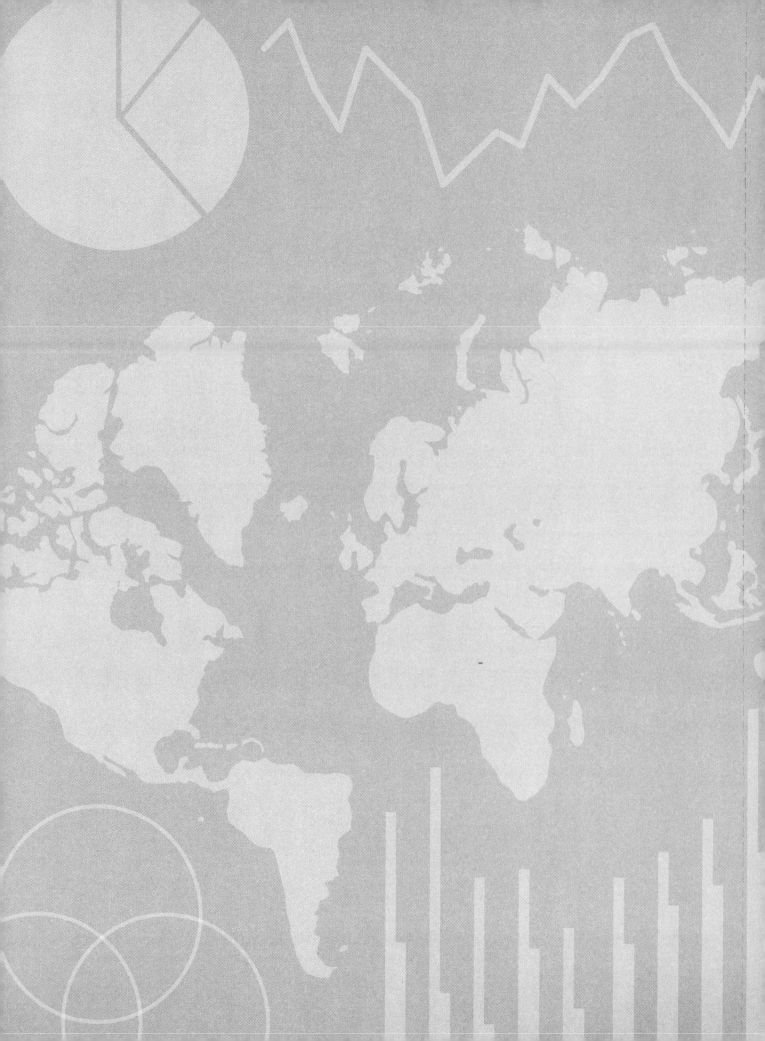

Make a Plan

Look at the book titles listed below. Each column shows books in a different genre. A *genre* is a type or category of book. Make a check mark in the box next to each book you plan to read.

Fiction	Historical Fiction	Poetry	Mystery	Biography
☐ *Flat Stanley: His Original Adventure* (Brown)	☐ *Keep the Lights Burning, Abbie* (Roop)	☐ *Where the Sidewalk Ends* (Silverstein)	☐ *Nate the Great* (Sharmat)	☐ *I Am Amelia Earhart* (Meltzer)
☐ *Poppleton and Friends* (Rylant)	☐ *Sam the Minuteman* (Benchley)	☐ *A Pizza the Size of the Sun* (Prelutsky)	☐ *The Boxcar Children (#1)* (Warner)	☐ *Snowflake Bentley* (Briggs Martin)
☐ *Ivy & Bean* (Barrows)	☐ *Dust for Dinner* (Turner)	☐ *Switching on the Moon* (Yolen and Peters)	☐ *Ballpark Mysteries #1: The Fenway Foul-up* (Kelly)	☐ *The Story of Ruby Bridges* (Coles)
☐ *Horrible Harry in Room 2B* (Kline)	☐ *Freedom Summer* (Wiles)	☐ *The Bill Martin Jr Big Book of Poetry* (Martin)	☐ *The Trouble with Chickens* (Cronin)	☐ *Wilma Unlimited* (Krull)
☐ *Owl at Home* (Lobel)	☐ *Small Wolf* (Benchley)	☐ *Once I Ate a Pie* (MacLachlan and Charest)	☐ *Minnie and Moo* (Cazet)	☐ *Manfish: A Story of Jacques Cousteau* (Berne)

Up, Up, and Away

Why does a balloon float?

Push a cork to the bottom of a bucket of water. When you let go, the cork rises to the top of the water. Why? The cork is less dense than the water. A piece of cork weighs less than an equal amount of water. Hot air, helium, and hydrogen rise for the same reason. All three gases are less dense than regular air. A balloon filled with hot air, helium, or hydrogen weighs less than an equal amount of regular air.

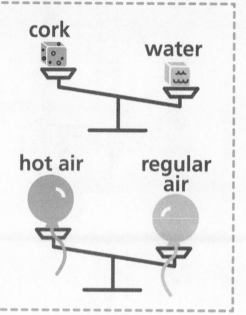

cork

water

hot air

regular air

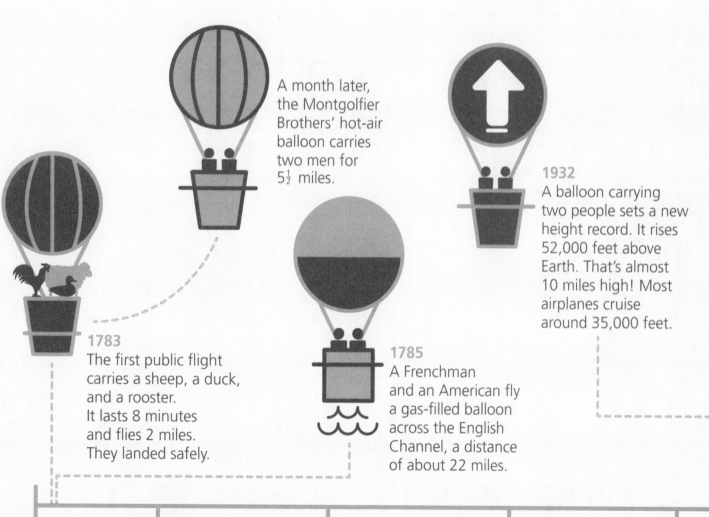

A month later, the Montgolfier Brothers' hot-air balloon carries two men for $5\frac{1}{2}$ miles.

1932
A balloon carrying two people sets a new height record. It rises 52,000 feet above Earth. That's almost 10 miles high! Most airplanes cruise around 35,000 feet.

1783
The first public flight carries a sheep, a duck, and a rooster. It lasts 8 minutes and flies 2 miles. They landed safely.

1785
A Frenchman and an American fly a gas-filled balloon across the English Channel, a distance of about 22 miles.

1780   1800   1830   1860   1890

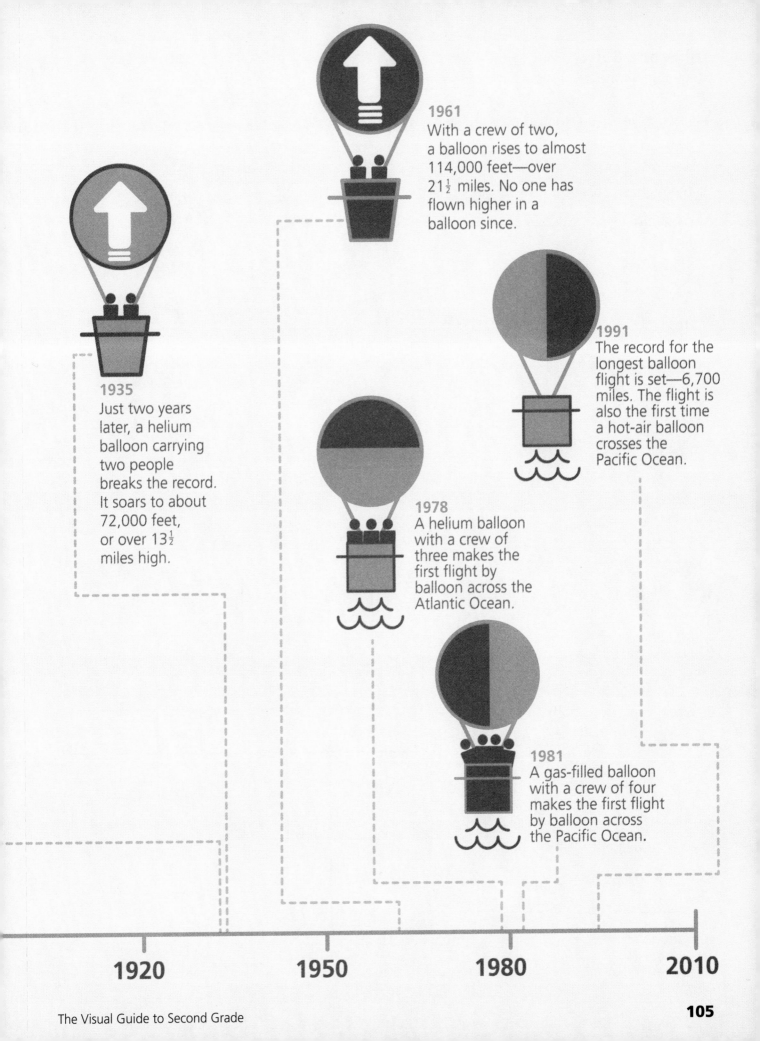

1961
With a crew of two, a balloon rises to almost 114,000 feet—over $21\frac{1}{2}$ miles. No one has flown higher in a balloon since.

1991
The record for the longest balloon flight is set—6,700 miles. The flight is also the first time a hot-air balloon crosses the Pacific Ocean.

1935
Just two years later, a helium balloon carrying two people breaks the record. It soars to about 72,000 feet, or over $13\frac{1}{2}$ miles high.

1978
A helium balloon with a crew of three makes the first flight by balloon across the Atlantic Ocean.

1981
A gas-filled balloon with a crew of four makes the first flight by balloon across the Pacific Ocean.

1920   **1950**   **1980**   **2010**

Think and Solve

Study the infographic. Answer the questions.

1. True or false? A balloon filled with hot air is denser than a balloon filled with cold air.

_____

2. The highest a balloon flew carrying a person

was more than _____ miles.

   A. 21

   B. 35

   C. 72

   D. 114

3. When did the first balloon cross the Pacific Ocean?

_____

4. Why does a cork float?

_____

Puzzle It

Read each clue below. Fill in the answers to complete the crossword puzzle.

Across

1. A cork will float in

_____.

5. What is the infographic's main idea? What is it mostly about?

6. What animal flew with a rooster and a duck on the first balloon flight?

Down

2. Which ocean was crossed in a helium balloon in 1978?

3. A balloon crossed the

_____ Channel in 1785.

4. Hydrogen is less _____ than regular air.

Explore Your World

Gather eight small objects from around the house. Make sure it is OK for the objects to get wet. Try to find things made of different materials: a metal object, a wooden object, a plastic object, and so on. Write the names of the objects on the lines in the chart below.

Which objects will float? Make a prediction and then test each one by dropping it in a tub full of water. Use the chart below to record your results.

Object	Prediction: Will it float?		Result: Did it float?		Is it more or less dense than water?	
1. _____	Yes	No	Yes	No	More	Less
2. _____	Yes	No	Yes	No	More	Less
3. _____	Yes	No	Yes	No	More	Less
4. _____	Yes	No	Yes	No	More	Less
5. _____	Yes	No	Yes	No	More	Less
6. _____	Yes	No	Yes	No	More	Less
7. _____	Yes	No	Yes	No	More	Less
8. _____	Yes	No	Yes	No	More	Less

Color It

Many hot-air balloons are colorful and interesting to look at. Color the patterns on these hot-air balloons. Draw your own pattern on the last balloon.

The Visual Guide to Second Grade

Ready, Set, Glow!

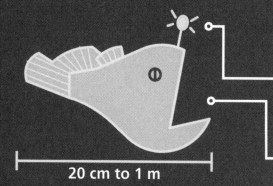

Anglerfish

Only females have a lighted "bait rod," used to attract prey.

They are so flexible and have such big mouths that they can eat prey up to twice their size!

20 cm to 1 m

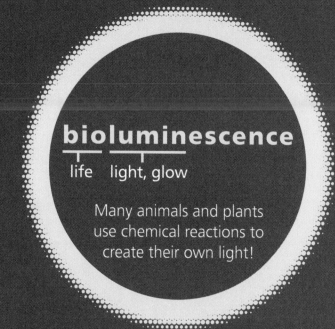

bioluminescence

life   light, glow

Many animals and plants use chemical reactions to create their own light!

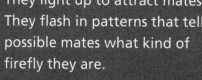

5 to 25 mm

Fireflies

They are also called *lightning bugs* and glow in a yellow color.

They light up to attract mates. They flash in patterns that tell possible mates what kind of firefly they are.

Mushrooms

More than 70 species glow in the dark!

They mainly glow to attract insects that will spread their spores.

In some mushrooms, only the caps or gills glow. In others, the stem glows.

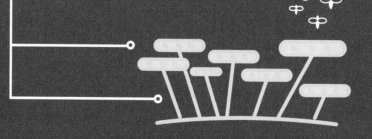

0.005 mm to 2 mm

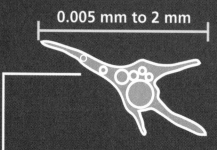

Dinoflagellates

They glow in a bluish-green color and sometimes make the ocean sparkle at night.

Large groups of them, called *blooms*, can cause red tides that change the color of the water and may poison fish.

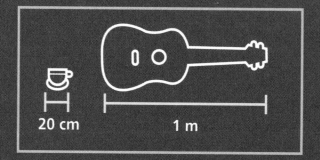

20 cm   1 m

108

Think and Solve

Study the infographic. Answer the questions.

1. Read the word. Circle the part of the word that means "light, glow."

bioluminescence

2. What causes some plants and animals to glow?
   A. heat
   B. chemical reactions
   C. reflecting sunlight
   D. reflecting moonlight

3. True or false? Fireflies glow to help them hunt for food at night.

_____

4. Number the animals from smallest to largest.
   _____ firefly _____ anglerfish _____ dinoflagellate

5. Large groups of dinoflagellates are called   _____.

Imagine It

Imagine you are a scientist who has discovered a new bioluminescent creature. In the box below, draw what it looks like. Then, write about the creature on the lines below. Where does the animal live? What body parts glow? Why does it glow?

_____

_____

_____

_____

_____

Money Museum

Who are those people on our coins and bills? Each one played an important role in American history.

$100 bill

Benjamin Franklin
Founding Father, First US Ambassador
to France, 1706–1790

$50 bill

Ulysses S. Grant
18th President of the United States,
1822–1885

$5 bill and 1¢ coin (penny)

Abraham Lincoln
16th President of the United States,
1809–1865

$2 bill and 5¢ coin (nickel)

Thomas Jefferson
3rd President of the United States,
1743–1826

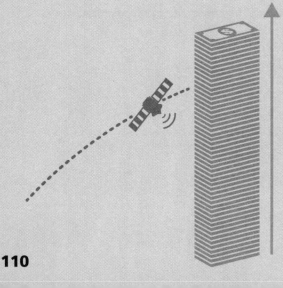

Paper money does not last long.
After about 5 years of use, a bill is
worn out and must be replaced. Old
paper money is shredded, or cut up
into tiny pieces. In 2010, about 6 billion
old bills were destroyed! That many
bills would make a stack more than
400 miles high, or higher than the
orbit of the Hubble telescope! Coins
last a much longer time. Most coins are
used for more than 20 years. When
coins are ready to be replaced,
the metal is recycled.

$20 bill

Andrew Jackson
7th President of the United States, 1767–1845

$10 bill

Alexander Hamilton
Founding Father, First US Secretary of the Treasury, 1755–1804

$1 bill and 25¢ coin (quarter)

George Washington
1st President of the United States, 1732–1799

Franklin D. Roosevelt
32nd President of the United States, 1882–1945

10¢ coin (dime)

John F. Kennedy
35th President of the United States, 1917–1963

50¢ coin (half-dollar)

Sacagawea
Native American Woman Who Traveled With Lewis and Clark, c.1788–1812

$1 coin (golden dollar)

Think and Solve

Study the infographic. Answer the questions.

1. Which man never served as president of the United States?

    A. Thomas Jefferson

    B. Benjamin Franklin

    C. Andrew Jackson

    D. Ulysses S. Grant

2. True or false? Abraham Lincoln was president before Ulysses S. Grant.

_____

3. How many old bills were destroyed in 2010?

    A. 6,000

    B. 6,000,000

    C. 6,000,000,000

    D. 600

4. Who was Sacagawea?

_____

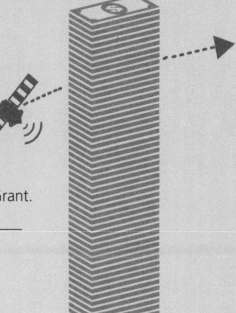

Do the Math

Javier has six different bills and coins. They total $26.31. Circle the bills and coins that he has.

Collect Data

Collect at least 30 coins of different types. How many of each coin do you have? Record the answers below.

pennies: _____   nickels: _____   dimes: _____

quarters: _____   half-dollars:_____   one-dollars:_____

Make a Bar Graph

Graph the data about your coins. Which coin do you have the most of? How many do you have? On the left side of the graph, write that number at the top. This is the highest amount to show on your graph. Above each type of coin, draw a bar that ends beside the number you have.

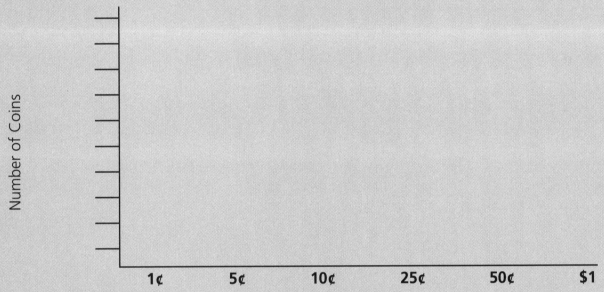

What is the total value of the coins you have? $ _____

Compare and Contrast

Look closely at the coins you found. Answer the questions.

Which coin is the oldest? Write the year and type of coin.

_____

Which coin is the newest? Write the year and type of coin.

_____

Find two coins that have the same value but look different. How are they different?

_____

How are they the same?

_____

Champion of Chimps

Scientist Jane Goodall has dedicated her life to studying chimpanzees in the wild.

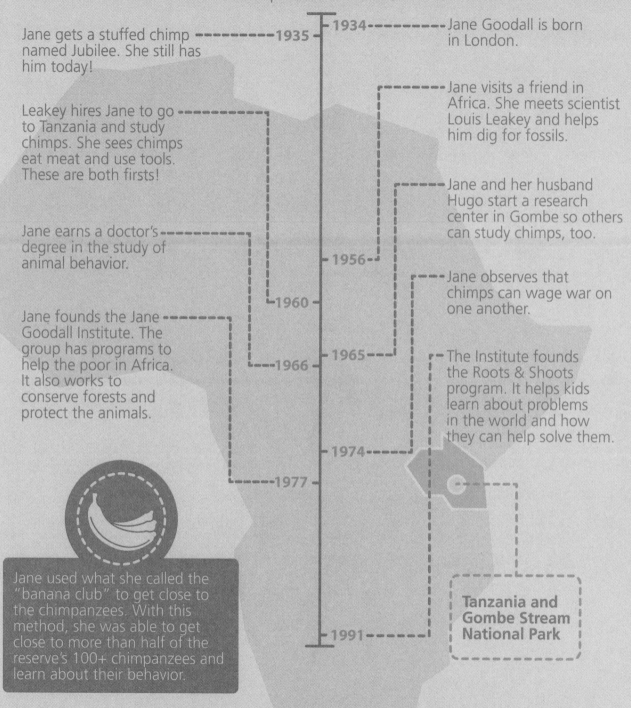

1935 — Jane gets a stuffed chimp named Jubilee. She still has him today!

1934 — Jane Goodall is born in London.

Jane visits a friend in Africa. She meets scientist Louis Leakey and helps him dig for fossils.

Leakey hires Jane to go to Tanzania and study chimps. She sees chimps eat meat and use tools. These are both firsts!

Jane and her husband Hugo start a research center in Gombe so others can study chimps, too.

Jane earns a doctor's degree in the study of animal behavior.

1956

Jane observes that chimps can wage war on one another.

1960

Jane founds the Jane Goodall Institute. The group has programs to help the poor in Africa. It also works to conserve forests and protect the animals.

1966

1965 — The Institute founds the Roots & Shoots program. It helps kids learn about problems in the world and how they can help solve them.

1974

1977

Tanzania and Gombe Stream National Park

1991

Jane used what she called the "banana club" to get close to the chimpanzees. With this method, she was able to get close to more than half of the reserve's 100+ chimpanzees and learn about their behavior.

Jane was one of the first scientists to give her subjects names.

- Passion
- Fifi
- Flint
- Goliath
- Flo
- Frodo

"We have a choice to use the gift of our lives to make the world a better place."
~ Dr. Jane Goodall

Piece It Together

Cut out the regions of Africa. On page 117, glue or tape the pieces together to show the whole continent. When you have completed the map, label the country Tanzania. Use the infographic to help you.

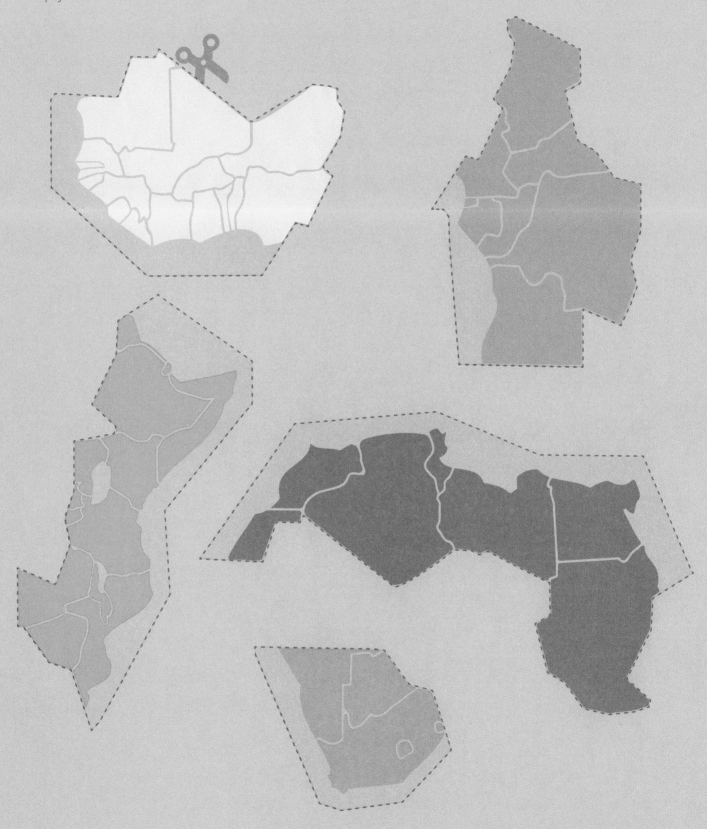

Map of Africa

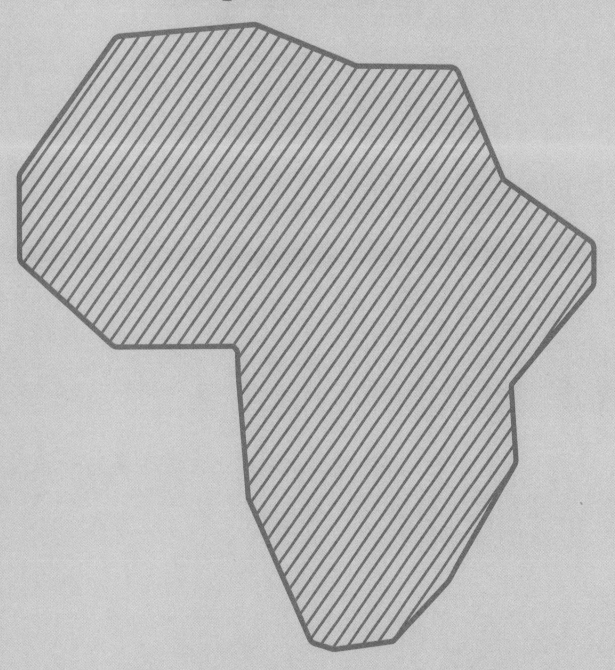

Keep on Brushing

5000 BC — Ancient Egyptians make a tooth powder. It has eggshells and ox hooves in it! They use their fingers to brush.

In Babylonia, a chewing stick is used to clean teeth. It is a twig with a frayed end. — **3500–3000 BC**

1600 BC — The Chinese make chewing sticks from good-smelling tree twigs.

Hog hairs and horse hairs were common choices for toothbrush bristles. You can still buy natural boar-bristle brushes today!

1690 — The first written use of the word *toothbrush*

William Addis makes the first modern toothbrush while he is in jail. It has a bone handle and boar bristles. — **1780**

1857 — H. N. Wadsworth gets the first US patent for toothbrushes.

DuPont starts to make brushes with nylon bristles. — **1937**

1940s — World War II soldiers bring home the habit of brushing to the US.

The first electric toothbrush (the Broxodent) is invented in Switzerland. — **1954**

1961 — The first cordless toothbrush is invented.

Sonic toothbrushes are introduced. They vibrate at 31,000 brush strokes per minute! — **1980s**

Americans say that the toothbrush is the number one invention they cannot live without.

The toothbrush company that William Addis started is still around today.

Think and Solve

Study the infographic. Answer the questions.

1. Soldiers in World War II got in the habit of brushing their teeth in the army. When they came

   home, they _____.

   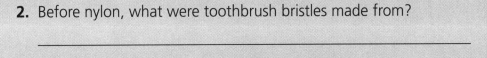

   A. could not buy toothpaste

   B. brought the habit with them

   C. did not bring their toothbrushes

   D. stopped brushing

2. Before nylon, what were toothbrush bristles made from?

   _____

3. The Chinese made chewing sticks from _____.

4. True or false? At one point in time, humans used their fingers as toothbrushes.

   _____

Log It

Each day, you should brush your teeth at least twice (in the morning and before bed). Each time you brush, you should keep brushing for two whole minutes. Keep track of how long you brush your teeth this week. Each empty hourglass is equal to two minutes of brushing. Color one hourglass for every two minutes you spend brushing.

Label It

The chart below shows baby teeth and their names. Read the labels on the right side of the mouth. Use them to help you label the teeth on the left side.

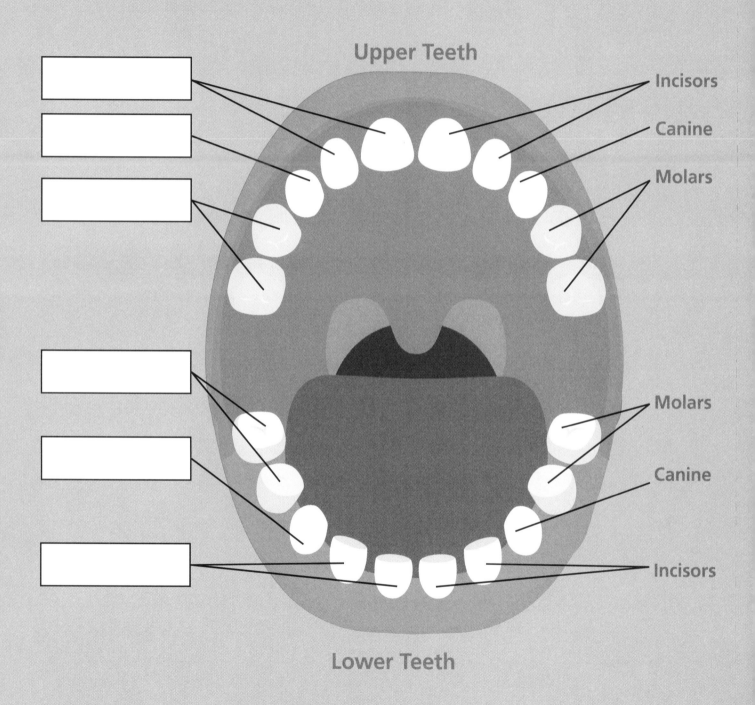

Upper Teeth

Incisors

Canine

Molars

Molars

Canine

Incisors

Lower Teeth

Use the diagram on page 120. Answer the questions.

1. How many baby teeth do humans have?

_____

2. True or false? The teeth on the left side of your mouth
are the same as on the right side.

_____

3. Do you have more incisors or canines?

_____

4. The teeth in the very back of your mouth are called _____.

  A. incisors

  B. molars

  C. canines

  D. fangs

5. Do you think you would be more likely to get a cavity in a canine or a molar? Why?

_____

_____

6. Circle the number that tells about how many baby teeth you have lost.

  0   1   3   5   7   9   12   15   18

7. What happens inside your mouth after you lose a baby tooth?

_____

Stars and Stripes

The American flag is a familiar sight. You see it at the post office, on the Fourth of July, and on front porches. What do you know about its history?

The 50 stars stand for the 50 states.

The stripes are also symbols for sunrays. Sunrays light up the world. America "lights up" the world with its ideas of freedom and democracy.

The flag's colors have special meanings. *
RED= hardiness and valor
WHITE = purity and innocence
BLUE= vigilance, perseverance, and justice

*In other words, bravery, goodness, and alertness, dedication, and fairness

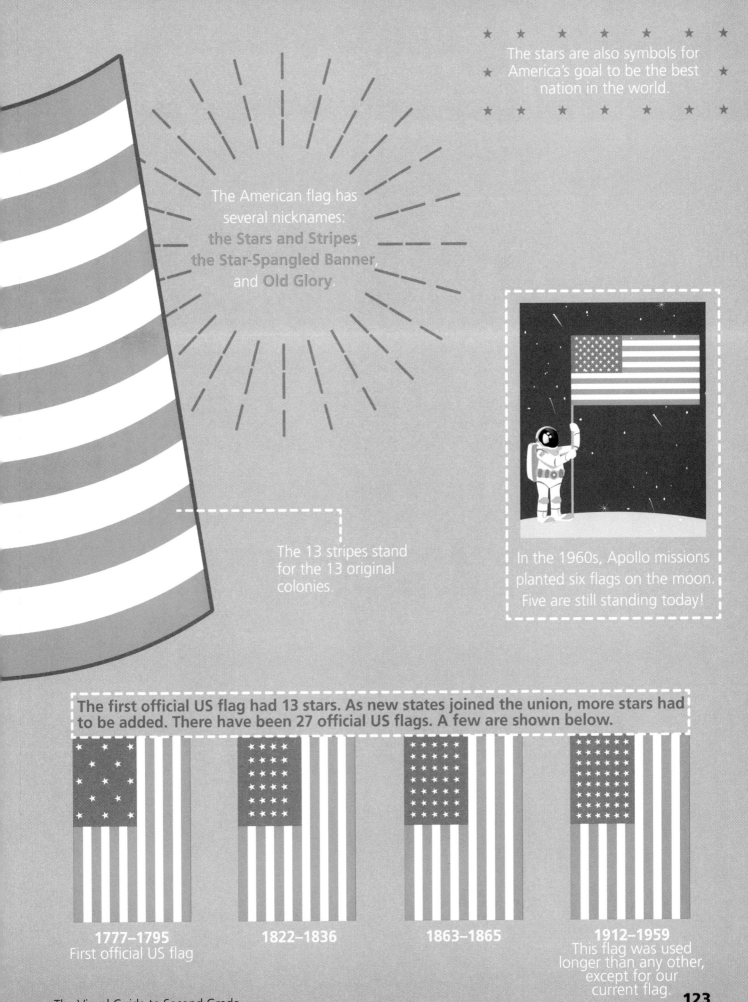

The stars are also symbols for America's goal to be the best nation in the world.

The American flag has several nicknames: the Stars and Stripes, the Star-Spangled Banner, and Old Glory.

The 13 stripes stand for the 13 original colonies.

In the 1960s, Apollo missions planted six flags on the moon. Five are still standing today!

The first official US flag had 13 stars. As new states joined the union, more stars had to be added. There have been 27 official US flags. A few are shown below.

1777–1795
First official US flag

1822–1836

1863–1865

1912–1959
This flag was used longer than any other, except for our current flag.

Think and Solve
Study the infographic. Answer the questions.

1. Alaska and Hawaii were the last two states to join the union. Did they become states before or after 1959? How do you know?

_____

_____

2. How many more stars did the 1863 flag have than the 1822 flag?

_____

3. Draw a line to match each color to what it symbolizes on the flag.

red   **caution, hard work, and fairness**

white   **strength and bravery**

blue   **honesty and innocence**

4. Which is not a nickname for the American flag?

A. the Stars and Stripes

B. the Star-Spangled Banner

C. Starry Night

D. Old Glory

5. _____American flags have been planted on the moon.

6. True or false? The first official US flag had 26 stars.

_____

Research and Report

This US map shows the date that each state became a part of the country. Look at the map. In the stars below, write the abbreviations for the first 13 states to become part of the United States of America. They should be in order by the date they joined the union.

Arctic or Antarctica?

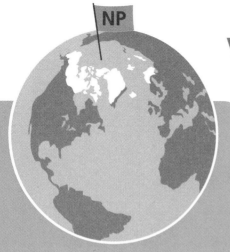

VS.

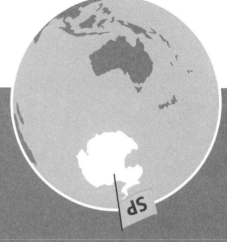

The Arctic

The Arctic is at the top of Earth. It is where you will find the North Pole.

Below the thick sheet of ice that covers the top of Earth is the Arctic Ocean. There is no land below the ice.

Parts of Canada, Russia, the USA, Greenland, Norway, Finland, Sweden, and Iceland are located in the Arctic.

Nearly 4 million people live in the Arctic.

On average, winter temperatures in the Arctic are –30°F (–34.4°C).

The explorer Robert Peary is usually given credit as the leader of the first expedition to reach the North Pole in 1909.

Polar bears, whales, seals, walruses, and Arctic foxes are a few of the many animals that make their home in the Arctic.

Antarctica

Antarctica is at the bottom of Earth. It is where you will find the South Pole.

Below the thick sheet of ice that covers the bottom of Earth is the continent of Antarctica. It is the fifth largest continent. It is bigger than both Europe and Australia.

No countries have land located in Antarctica.

About 5,000 people live in Antarctica during the summer. In winter, the population drops to 1,000 people.

On average, winter temperatures in Antarctica are –56°F (–48.8°C).

The explorer Roald Amundsen led the first expedition to reach the South Pole in 1911.

Penguins, whales, seals, and many types of seabirds make their home in Antarctica. There are no land mammals that live in Antarctica.

-30°F

-56°F

Think and Solve

Study the infographic. Answer the questions.

1. True or false? There are no land mammals living in Antarctica.

_____

2. The _____ Ocean is below the ice sheet that covers the Arctic.

3. Robert Peary reached the _____ Pole in 1909.

4. Which is colder, the Arctic or Antarctica?

_____

Compare and Contrast

Read the facts. If a fact tells only about the Arctic, write it in the left circle. If a fact tells only about Antarctica, write it in the right circle. If the fact tells about both places, write it in the middle.

polar bears live there   **countries have land there**   **no countries have land there**

covered in an ice sheet   **land beneath the ice sheet**   **where the North Pole is**

people live there   **where the South Pole is**   **whales live there**

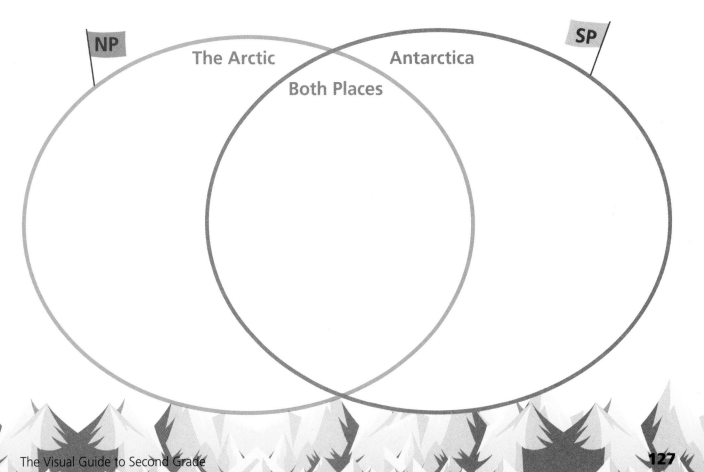

Bottles, Bottles Everywhere

50 billion

water bottles
bought each year

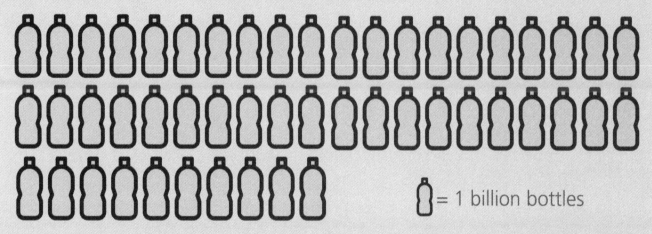

= 1 billion bottles

=

17 million

barrels of oil
needed to make them

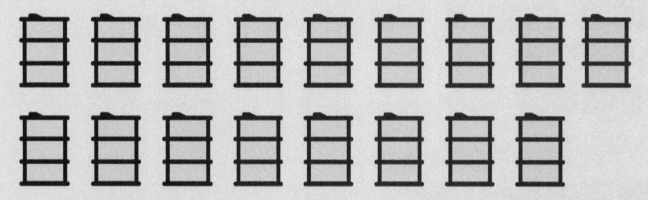

= 1 million barrels of oil

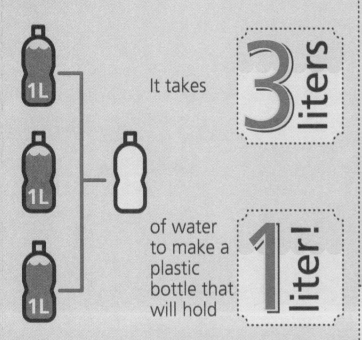

It takes **3 liters** of water to make a plastic bottle that will hold **1 liter!**

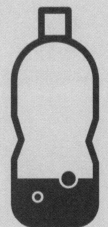

Fill a water bottle ¼ full of oil. That is about how much oil was used to make the bottle!

Look for a number in a triangle. The number tells you what kind of plastic it is. In most places, you can recycle numbers 1 and 2 plastics.

- drink bottles
- peanut butter containers

- milk jugs
- some trash and plastic bags

- cleaning bottles
- clear food packaging

- squeezable bottles
- dry cleaning bags

- ketchup bottles
- bottle caps

- disposable plates
- egg cartons

- five-gallon bottles
- DVDs

Only 1 out of 5

water bottles are recycled. The rest end up buried in landfills—or littering the world.

cost of drinking tap water for 1 year = **50¢**

cost of drinking the same amount of bottled water for 1 year = **$1,000** or more

Think and Solve

Study the infographic. Answer the questions.

1. True or false? Only Number 1 plastic can be recycled.

_____

2. A store sells 5,000 water bottles in one month. How many of those water bottles can be recycled?

_____

About how many of the water bottles will be recycled?

_____

About how many will be buried in a landfill?

_____

3. Write 0 on each line below to show the number of water bottles sold each year.

5, _____   _____   _____,   _____   _____   _____,   _____   _____   _____

4. Most things made of plastic are marked with a number in a triangle. What does the number tell you?

   A. the type of plastic

   B. where the plastic was made

   C. how many times the plastic can be recycled

   D. all of the above

5. If you drink only tap water for three years, about how much will you spend on drinking water?

   A. 50¢

   B. $1.25

   C. $1.50

   D. $3.00

Read About It:
How Are Plastic Bottles Made?

MOST PLASTIC BOTTLES are made from natural gas or oil. At a chemical plant, the gas or oil is made into tiny pellets of plastic. Each piece is about the size of a grain of rice. These tiny pieces are shipped to factories that make bottles. At the factory, the pellets are melted and shaped. The shape looks sort of like a balloon that is not blown up yet. When the plastic shape is still warm and soft, it is put into a mold. The mold is shaped like a water bottle. The soft plastic is blown up with air. It fills the mold and becomes shaped like a bottle. Once it cools down and hardens, it is filled with water.

Make Idea Webs
Review the infographic and the passage above. Think about times you have used plastic water bottles. What are some good reasons to use plastic water bottles? What are some reasons to avoid using plastic water bottles? Fill in the idea webs. Write a reason on each line.

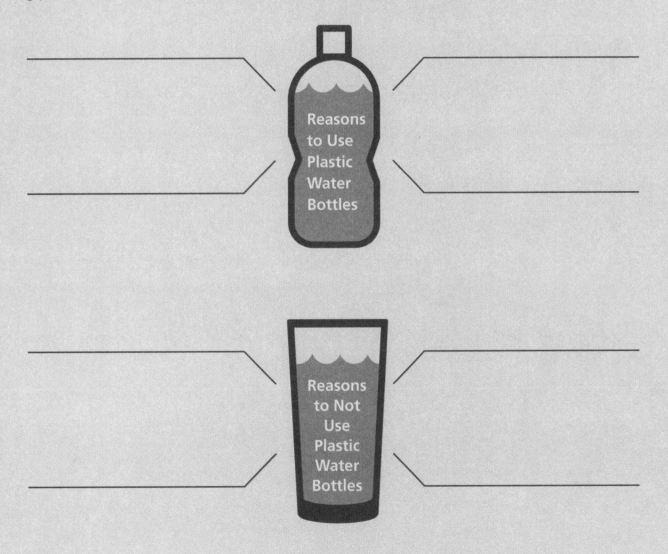

A Home Run for History

Jackie Robinson was a true American hero. His accomplishments on the baseball diamond made him famous and inspired others. Even after his sports career ended, he worked hard to ensure equality for all.

Jackie volunteered for the National Association for the Advancement of Colored People (NAACP). Throughout his life, he worked to help integrate (join) people of all races in sports and in every part of life.

42

Jackie's baseball uniform number (42) was retired in his honor. No other player in Major League Baseball will use it.

Major League Baseball, or MLB, has been around since 1869. Players in MLB are professional, or paid, athletes. Until 1947, the MLB only allowed white players. Back then, if black people wanted to be paid to play baseball, they joined the Negro Leagues. Today, Major League Baseball has athletes of all different races.

Jackie played in the World Series six times! In 1949, he won the MLB MVP (Most Valuable Player) Award. He was voted into the Baseball Hall of Fame in 1962.

Jackie Robinson made history when he became the first African American to play Major League Baseball in 1947. That same year, he won the first-ever MLB Rookie of the Year Award.

1919
Jackie is born in Georgia.

1940
Jackie excels at football, baseball, basketball, and track while at college.

1945
Jackie plays baseball in the Negro Leagues.

1947
Jackie is hired by the Brooklyn Dodgers, an MLB team.

1950
Jackie stars in a movie about himself!

1955
Jackie and the Dodgers win the World Series.

1957
Jackie retires from baseball.

1963
Jackie marches with Martin Luther King, Jr. for civil rights in Alabama.

1972
Jackie dies.

Think and Solve
Study the infographic. Answer the questions.

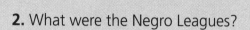

1. True or false? Jackie Robinson won the first MLB Rookie of the Year Award.

_____

2. What were the Negro Leagues?

_____

3. True or false? Jackie Robinson starred in a movie about himself after he retired from baseball.

_____

4. What is the NAACP?

_____

_____

5. Which sport is not listed as one Jackie played?

   A. track

   B. basketball

   C. football

   D. soccer

6. How old was Jackie when he died?

_____

7. What do you think it means to "retire" a player's uniform number?

_____

_____

Write About It

In the space below, write a summary of Jackie Robinson's greatest accomplishments.

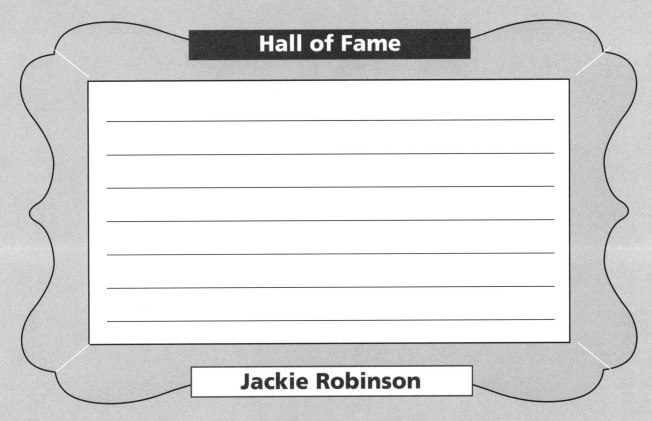

Imagine yourself far in the future. What have your accomplishments been? What did you do to be voted into a Hall of Fame? Write a summary of your greatest accomplishments below.

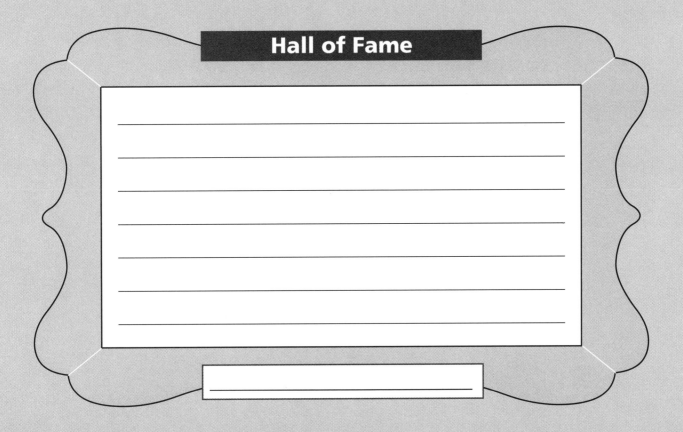

Standing Up to Bullies

Do you know someone who is a bully? Have you ever been bullied? Most people meet a bully at some point in their lives. Bullying isn't right, and no one deserves it. By learning more about it, you'll know what to do the next time you see a bully in action.

9. Don't go places alone—especially places you've been bullied.

10. Stand up for others.

name-calling shoving gossiping
leaving out threatening
BULLYING
embarrassing in public spreading rumors
ganging up taunting
tripping kicking
posting hurtful things online

8. Don't bottle up your feelings. Talk to someone you trust.

7. Don't show the bully how you feel.

6. Act confidently.

1 in 7 students is either a bully or gets bullied.

1.
Talk to an adult. If he or she can't help, tell someone else.

3.2 million
kids a year are bullied.

2.
Ignore the bully.

insulting
pushing
damaging property
**playing
mean
jokes**
controlling
teasing meanly
hitting

power
lying

3.
Don't respond with violence.

There are many types of bullying. They all involve trying to show power over someone else. The words in the cloud are related to bullying. Can you think of any others?

4.
Try to turn a comment into a joke.

5.
Walk away.

Telling vs. Tattling

Don't be afraid to tell an adult about bullying. Telling and tattling aren't the same. Telling an adult protects you or someone else. Tattling is done to get someone in trouble.

Think and Solve

Study the infographic. Answer the questions.

1. True or false? Telling and tattling are the same thing.

_____

2. What are three examples of bullying?

_____   _____   _____

3. If you are being bullied, the most important thing to do is _____.

    A. ignore it

    B. get revenge

    C. bottle up your feelings

    D. tell an adult

Read About It:
Stopping Bullies in the Act

Read each scene. On the lines, write advice you would give to the child who is being bullied.

MAGGIE IS NEW AT SCHOOL. At lunch, she holds her tray and looks for somewhere to sit. She sees some girls from her class. Maggie asks if she can sit with them. One girl, Jaden, smirks at Maggie. "Sorry," she says, in a singsong voice. "These seats are all taken." She turns her back to Maggie and laughs with her friends.

_____

_____

_____

_____

_____

_____

IT IS SATURDAY MORNING. Antonio has baseball practice. He doesn't have any friends on the team yet. He is hoping today will be better. The coach talks to the team. Then, he tells the outfielders to take the field. Connor sticks out his foot, and Antonio trips. Connor kicks some dirt at Antonio as he walks past. A couple of the other boys laugh. No one offers Antonio a hand.

_____

_____

_____

_____

_____

_____

MAYA IS HANGING UP HER JACKET. She is early today, and she is alone in the coatroom. "Hey!" says a voice. It's Brendan. Maya looks at the ground. She knows what he's going to say. "Where's your lunch money?" he asks. "You owe me yesterday's, too."

Maya is silent for a minute. "I won't have anything to eat," she says finally.

"Not my problem," says Brendan. "Hurry up!" he orders, stepping closer.

A Natural Wonder

The Grand Canyon began to form 6 million years ago. Year by year, the Colorado River slowly carried away rocks and dirt. After millions of years, the river has carved a deep, wide canyon through the landscape. Today, the Grand Canyon is a popular place to visit. About 5 million people go there every year!

18 miles

The Grand Canyon is 18 miles across at its widest point.

The deepest part of the Grand Canyon is 6,000 feet deep. You would need to stack almost 5 Empire State Buildings to reach the top!

The Grand Canyon is 277 miles long. That's almost as long as the state of Pennsylvania!

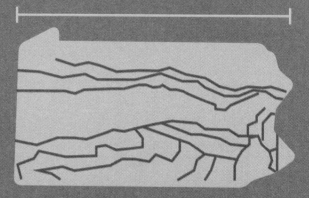

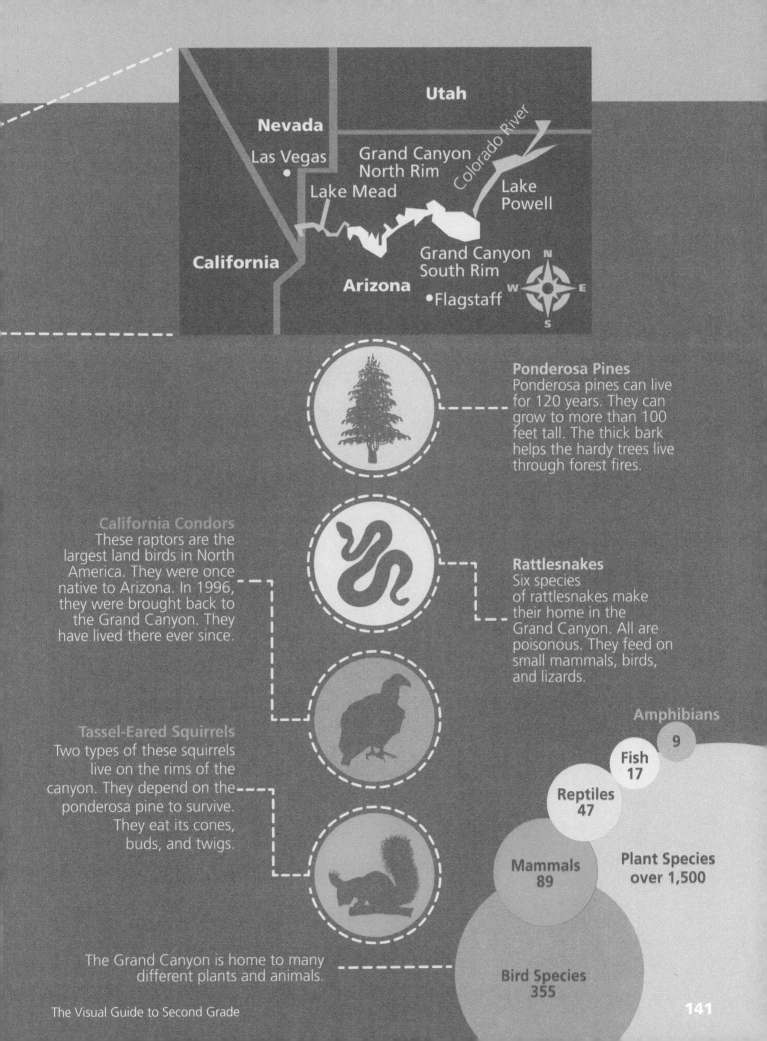

Utah

Nevada

Las Vegas

Grand Canyon
North Rim

Colorado River

Lake Mead

Lake
Powell

California

Grand Canyon
South Rim

Arizona

•Flagstaff

N
W E
S

Ponderosa Pines
Ponderosa pines can live for 120 years. They can grow to more than 100 feet tall. The thick bark helps the hardy trees live through forest fires.

California Condors
These raptors are the largest land birds in North America. They were once native to Arizona. In 1996, they were brought back to the Grand Canyon. They have lived there ever since.

Rattlesnakes
Six species of rattlesnakes make their home in the Grand Canyon. All are poisonous. They feed on small mammals, birds, and lizards.

Amphibians
9

Fish
17

Reptiles
47

Tassel-Eared Squirrels
Two types of these squirrels live on the rims of the canyon. They depend on the ponderosa pine to survive. They eat its cones, buds, and twigs.

Mammals
89

Plant Species
over 1,500

The Grand Canyon is home to many different plants and animals.

Bird Species
355

Think and Solve

Study the infographic. Answer the questions.

1. Which lake is located west of the Grand Canyon?

_____

2. Can ponderosa pines live for longer than one century?

_____

3. The Grand Canyon is located in _____.
   A. Colorado
   B. Utah
   C. Arizona
   D. Connecticut

4. Rounded to the nearest ten, the Grand Canyon is_____ miles across at its widest point.

Write About It

Pretend you are visiting the Grand Canyon.
On the back of the postcard below,
write a note to a friend.

Piece It Together

Cut out the canyon labels. Glue or tape them to the map on page 145 to show where they are found in the world. The numbers will help you place them correctly. (Note: *Gorge* is another name for *canyon*.)

1. Tiger Leaping Gorge (China)

one of the deepest canyons in the world

2. Gorges du Verdon (France)

known for the beautiful green color of the water

3. Antelope Canyon (Arizona, USA)

flowing shapes in the sandstone were formed

by floods and heavy rains

4. Copper Canyon (Mexico)

fun to view from a railroad that runs

through bridges and tunnels

5. Waimea Canyon (Hawaii)

largest canyon in the Pacific; known

for its lovely colors

6. Indus Gorge (Pakistan)

the deepest canyon in the world at about 17,000 feet

7. Fjaðrárgljúfur Canyon (Iceland)

made by flowing water from glaciers

Canyons of the World

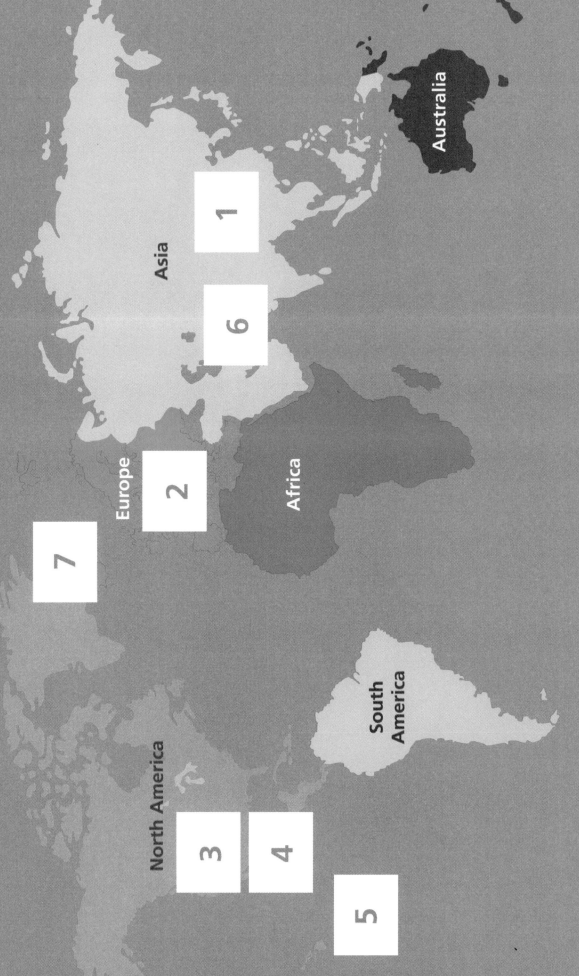

Australia

Asia

Europe

Africa

South America

North America

1

6

2

7

3

4

5

Roller Coasters

Zoom up! Zoom down! Zoom upside-down! A roller coaster ride is a wild, fun time. In most amusement parks, the roller coasters are the stars. But who first came up with the idea?

1400s Wooden sleds were raced down icy mountains. The sleds were called *flying mountains*. They reached speeds of up to 50 miles per hour.

1885 Phillip Hinkle made the first roller coaster like the ones we know today. It had a large hill at the start. A chain pulled the cars to the top of the hill. Then, the cars went zooming down and around the track.

1870 A scenic railway in Pennsylvania took thrill seekers for a wild ride. Each passenger paid a nickel. The riders saw the Pocono Mountains and a mine that was on fire. But they had to look quickly. The train went as fast as 65 miles an hour.

1895 Lina Beecher turned roller coaster fans upside-down. His Flip-Flap Railway was built on Coney Island near New York City. It had a 25-foot loop shaped like a circle. There are no coasters today with circle-shaped loops.

1976 The Great American Revolution opened. It is a roller coaster at Six Flags Magic Mountain in California. It was the first coaster with a loop shaped like an oval. The oval loop is safer than a loop shaped like a circle. Today, almost all amusement parks have a looping roller coaster.

A Coaster Dictionary

- **inversion:** the part of a roller coaster ride that turns riders upside-down
- **air time:** the feeling of floating that a rider feels when a coaster goes over a hill
- **flume:** a coaster that has small boats on water instead of cars on a track
- **mega coaster:** a roller coaster 150 to 220 feet tall
- **hyper coaster:** a roller coaster 200 feet or taller
- **giga coaster:** a roller coaster 300 feet or taller
- **strata coaster:** a roller coaster 400 feet or taller

1928 The Wildcat was built in Pennsylvania. It was the steepest wooden roller coaster of all time. The Wildcat's first hill was over 90 feet high. Riders screamed as the cars zoomed down at a 60-degree angle!

1966 The first flume ride was built at Six Flags over Texas.

1959 The Matterhorn was built in Disneyland®. It was the first steel roller coaster.

Think and Solve

Study the infographic. Answer the questions.

1. Phillip Hinkle built the first _____.

   A. looping roller coaster

   B. roller coaster like the ones we see today

   C. steel roller coaster

   D. flume

2. True or false? The Matterhorn was the first looping roller coaster built at Disneyland.

   _____

3. Why are there no more roller coasters with loops shaped like circles?

   _____

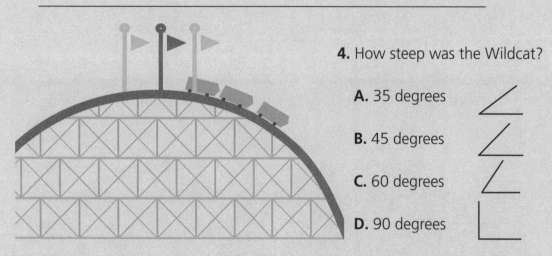

4. How steep was the Wildcat?

   A. 35 degrees

   B. 45 degrees

   C. 60 degrees

   D. 90 degrees

Match It

Draw a line from each coaster on the left to its description on the right.

strata coaster	**a roller coaster 300 feet or taller**
mega coaster	**a roller coaster 150 feet to 220 feet tall**
giga coaster	**a roller coaster 400 feet or taller**
hyper coaster	**a ride like a roller coaster, but with boats and water**
flume	**a roller coaster 200 feet or taller**

Imagine It

Imagine you are a roller coaster engineer. Your job is to design a new coaster. What will it look like? What special features will it have? In the box below, draw your roller coaster. Then, use the lines to tell about it.

Roller Coaster Name: _____

Roller Coaster Description:

_____

_____

_____

_____

The amusement park will advertise your new coaster. They need a slogan to put in the ads. Write a one-line slogan to make people excited to ride the new roller coaster.

_____

Digging Deep!

MANTLE

- about 1,800 miles thick
- made of rock
- some of the rock is liquid because it is so hot

CRUST

- about 5–25 miles thick
- thicker below land, thinner below oceans
- solid

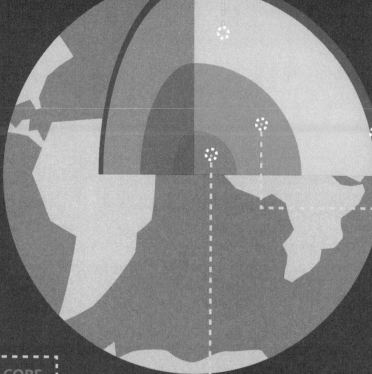

OUTER CORE

- about 1,400 miles thick
- liquid layer of mostly iron and nickel
- about 7,000°–9,000°F

INNER CORE

- the center of Earth
- an iron and nickel ball about 1,500 miles wide (That's about the distance from Florida to Vermont!)
- solid, not liquid, because of the pressure

VT

FL

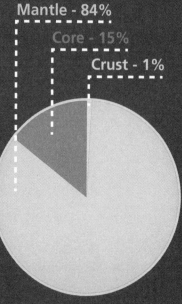

Mantle - 84%

Core - 15%

Crust - 1%

How Do We Know What's Inside?

Learning about what is inside Earth is no easy job. Geologists can drill into the crust. They can get a sample and study it. They can't drill deeper than the crust, though. Instead, scientists study waves from earthquakes. They learn about Earth's layers by watching how the waves change.

Think and Solve

Study the infographic. Answer the questions.

1. Which layer is thicker—the crust or the mantle?

_____

2. True or false? Geologists can't drill deeper than Earth's crust.

_____

3. The center of Earth is called the _____.

4. Earth's inner core is made of _____.

    A. diamonds

    B. iron and nickel

    C. oxygen and nickel

    D. hot lava

Try It Yourself

Make your own three-dimensional model of Earth's layers. Follow the directions.

1. You will need modeling clay in five different colors, including green and blue. You will also need a ruler with centimeter measurements.

2. Make three balls. The first should be about 1 cm across. It will be Earth's inner core.

3. Next, make a ball about 3 cm across for the outer core.

4. Make the third ball about 6 cm across. This is the mantle.

5. Cover the inner core with the outer core.

6. Cover the outer core with the mantle.

7. Last, make a thick layer of blue and green over the mantle. This is Earth's crust.

8. Ask an adult to carefully cut open your Earth to see its layers.

Nature's Skyscrapers

Feet

Many types of trees grow over 100 feet tall, towering high above Earth. This graph shows the tallest tree measured for each species.

380 feet

327 feet

318 feet

312 feet

Grows in:
US,
California

Grows in:
Australia

Grows in:
US,
Oregon

Grows in:
US,
California

Coast Redwood   **Mountain Ash**   **Sitka Spruce**   **Giant Sequoia**

295 feet

Coast redwoods are Earth's tallest trees. They can live for 2,000 years! These giants often grow taller than a 30-story building. Redwoods grow along the west coast of the US. The tallest are found in California. The locations of the four largest trees are kept a secret. This helps to keep them safe from harm. Each of these four special trees has a name that comes from Greek mythology: Hyperion (380 feet), Helios (374 feet), Icarus (371 feet), and Daedalus (363 feet). We must do our best to protect these giants of nature.

120 feet

100 feet

Grows in:
Papua New
Guinea

Grows in:
Eastern US

Grows in:
Eastern and
Midwestern US

6 feet

Klinki Pine   **Sweetgum**   **Pin Oak**   **Person**

Do the Math
Solve the problems. Use the infographic to help you.

1. How many feet taller is the tallest mountain ash than the tallest klinki pine?

_____feet

2. If the tallest pin oak and the tallest sitka spruce were stacked together, how tall would the stack be?

_____feet

3. How many feet taller is the tallest giant sequoia than the tallest sweetgum?

_____feet

4. If the tallest pin oak were measured in ten sections, how long would each section be?

_____feet

5. How many six-foot people would need to be stacked to match the height of the tallest sitka spruce?

_____six-foot people

Explore Your World
Is there a tall tree in your yard, in your neighborhood, or in a nearby park? Did you ever wonder how tall the tree is? Follow these steps to find out.

1. Choose the tree you want to measure.

2. Turn your back to the tree and bend down. Look through your legs at the tree.

3. Move closer or farther away until you can see the tree from top to bottom between your legs.

4. When you have found the right spot, turn around.

5. Mark your spot and measure the distance to the tree in feet. This distance will be about the height of the tree.

Make a Chart

Choose five tall things you would like to measure. They might be trees, buildings, basketball hoops, telephone poles, or street signs. Write the name of each item on a line in the chart. Draw each item. Then, use the steps on page 154 to estimate the height of the item in feet.

Item	Drawing	Estimated Height in Feet
_____		
_____		
_____		
_____		
_____		

Who Was Teddy Roosevelt?

Theodore Roosevelt was the youngest president ever. He took office in 1901 after President William McKinley died. Roosevelt was just 42 years old when he became the nation's 26th president. He was a great leader, but *leader* is only one of many words that describe him.

"Do what you can with what you have, where you are."

"Speak softly and carry a big stick; you will go far."

"Keep your eyes on the stars and your feet on the ground."

"Believe you can and you're halfway there."

"A grove of giant redwoods or sequoias should be kept just as we keep a great and beautiful cathedral."

"The only man who never makes a mistake is the man who never does anything."

Teddy Roosevelt was a wise man. He was always ready to share his ideas with others. Here are a few of his greatest quotes.

Peaceful
Roosevelt won the Nobel Peace Prize in 1906. He helped end the Russo-Japanese War.

Adventurous
Roosevelt was the first president to leave the US while in office. In 1906, he boarded a boat to inspect the construction of the Panama Canal.

Stubborn
Little "Teedie" was sick as a child. He had asthma and was skinny and weak. That just made him determined. He learned to box and began to work out. The rest of his life, he was a big fan of exercise. He even climbed the Swiss Alps!

Caring
Roosevelt created the first US wildlife refuge on Pelican Island in Florida. He wanted to protect tropical birds that were hunted for their feathers. Today, there are more than 500 US refuges.

Brave
Roosevelt fought in the Spanish-American War. He led a group of soldiers on horseback. They were called the *Rough Riders*. He was named a national hero after the war.

Book-Loving
Roosevelt loved to read and write. During his life, he wrote 38 books!

Tough
Roosevelt was shot in 1912 just before giving a speech. He decided to give the speech anyway. He spoke for 90 minutes with a bullet in his chest!

Generous
Roosevelt was the father of six children. Being a father was his favorite role in life. When he had to be away, he wrote his sons and daughters wonderful letters. He always took time to play, hike, read, and swim with them.

TEDDY BEARS were named after Roosevelt. On a hunting trip, he did not shoot a bear that had been captured and tied to a tree. A store owner heard the story. He asked if he could name a toy bear "Teddy's Bear." The name caught on and is still used today.

Think and Solve

Study the infographic. Answer the questions.

1. True or false? Teddy Roosevelt was the youngest person to become president.

   _____

2. Roosevelt led soldiers on horseback during _____.

   A. the Civil War

   B. the War of 1812

   C. World War I

   D. the Spanish-American War

3. According to the infographic, why was Roosevelt stubborn?

   _____

   _____

4. What kind of building did Roosevelt compare a redwood forest to?

   _____

5. Adjectives are describing words. The infographic lists eight adjectives that describe Teddy Roosevelt. Write one more adjective that describes Roosevelt and tell why you think it is true.

   _____

   _____

   _____

6. Which is not one of Roosevelt's accomplishments?

   A. winning the Nobel Peace Prize

   B. creating the first wildlife refuge in the US

   C. traveling to the North Pole

   D. climbing the Swiss Alps

Read About It:
Roosevelt's Gifts to the Future

TEDDY ROOSEVELT LOVED THE OUTDOORS. He knew that the US was rich in natural and wild places. He also understood that these special areas needed to be protected. Otherwise, they would not be there in the future. While he was president, Roosevelt set aside 230 million acres of land to be protected.

He created five National Parks. The first was Crater Lake National Park in Oregon in 1902. He also created 18 National Monuments, including Natural Bridges in Utah. Another National Monument he created was the Grand Canyon. Later, it became a National Park.

Forests were protected by Roosevelt as well. He created 150 National Forests! Tongass National Forest in Alaska is the largest National Forest in the US. It was created by Roosevelt in 1907.

Roosevelt loved all wildlife, but birds in particular. He created 51 Bird Reserves during his presidency. These were the first wildlife refuges in the US. Today, there are more than 500!

List It

Review the infographic and the passage above. Then, for each category, write an example of a natural protected area that Roosevelt created.

National Monument: _____

National Forest: _____

National Park: _____

National Wildlife Refuge: _____

What kind of park or animal preserve would you create? Write to describe it.

_____

_____

_____

The United States of Food

Top Food Crops by State

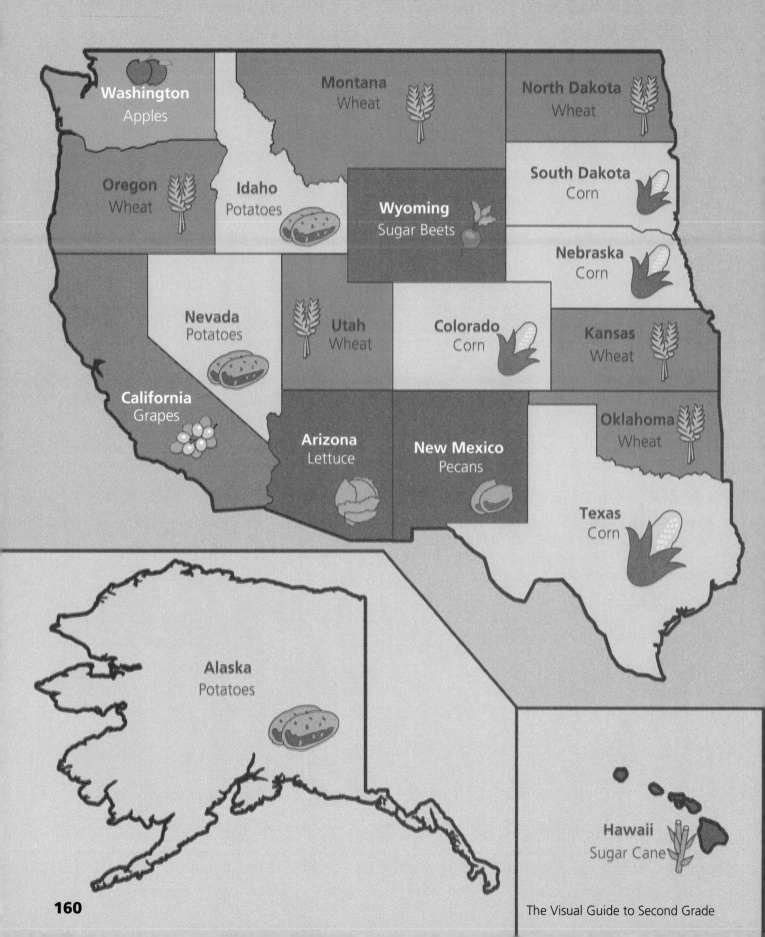

Washington
Apples

Montana
Wheat

North Dakota
Wheat

Oregon
Wheat

Idaho
Potatoes

Wyoming
Sugar Beets

South Dakota
Corn

Nebraska
Corn

Nevada
Potatoes

Utah
Wheat

Colorado
Corn

Kansas
Wheat

California
Grapes

Arizona
Lettuce

New Mexico
Pecans

Oklahoma
Wheat

Texas
Corn

Alaska
Potatoes

Hawaii
Sugar Cane

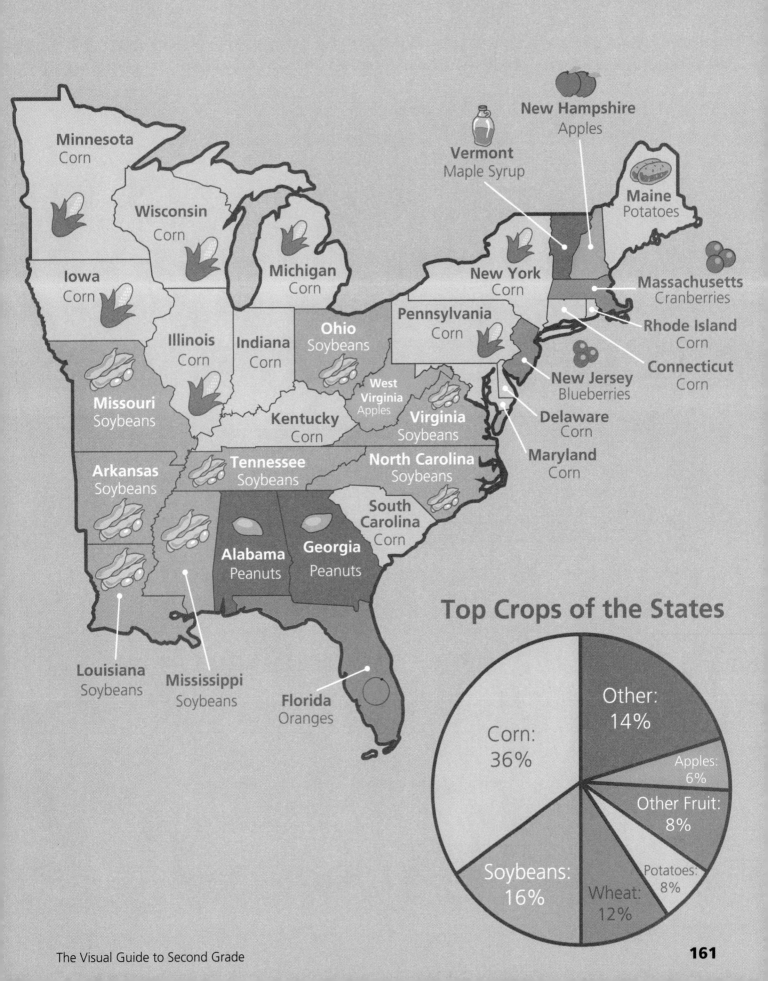

New Hampshire
Apples

Vermont
Maple Syrup

Maine
Potatoes

Minnesota
Corn

Wisconsin
Corn

Michigan
Corn

New York
Corn

Massachusetts
Cranberries

Iowa
Corn

Illinois
Corn

Indiana
Corn

Ohio
Soybeans

Pennsylvania
Corn

Rhode Island
Corn

Connecticut
Corn

West
Virginia
Apples

Virginia
Soybeans

New Jersey
Blueberries

Delaware
Corn

Maryland
Corn

Missouri
Soybeans

Kentucky
Corn

Arkansas
Soybeans

Tennessee
Soybeans

North Carolina
Soybeans

South
Carolina
Corn

Alabama
Peanuts

Georgia
Peanuts

Louisiana
Soybeans

Mississippi
Soybeans

Florida
Oranges

Top Crops of the States

Other:
14%

Apples:
6%

Other Fruit:
8%

Potatoes:
8%

Wheat:
12%

Corn:
36%

Soybeans:
16%

Think and Solve

Study the infographic. Answer the questions.

1. Which three states have apples as their top crop?

_____ _____ _____

2. The top crop for most states is _____.

    A. wheat

    B. corn

    C. soybeans

    D. potatoes

3. What percentage of states grow wheat or corn as their top crop?

_____%

4. Name three crops that are included in the category *Other* in the pie chart.

_____ _____ _____

5. Potatoes are the top crop grown in _____ of the states.

    A. 8%

    B. 12%

    C. 18%

    D. 6%

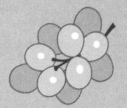

6. What is the top crop in your state?

_____

7. Describe another way the information in the infographic could be presented.

_____

_____

Make a Chart

In the chart below, show how many states grow each crop. For each crop, make a tally mark to show how many states grow it as their top crop. Count the tally marks in each row and write the total.

Examples:

| = 1 |||| = 5 |||| ||| = 8

Top Crop	Number of States	Total
Corn		
Soybeans		
Wheat		
Fruit		
Peanuts		

Which crop is the top crop in the most states? _____

Which crop is the top crop in the fewest states? _____

Write About It

Meadowview Elementary School

Lunch Menu for Tuesday, September 23:

Peanut Butter and Grape Jelly Sandwich on Wheat Bread

Popcorn

Apple

Read the lunch menu. Where did the ingredients come from? Write about the states where the foods and ingredients might have been grown.

_____

_____

_____

_____

_____

_____

_____

Stretching the Dollar

Over time, the cost of everything goes up. People earn more, but they must also pay more for the things they need and want.

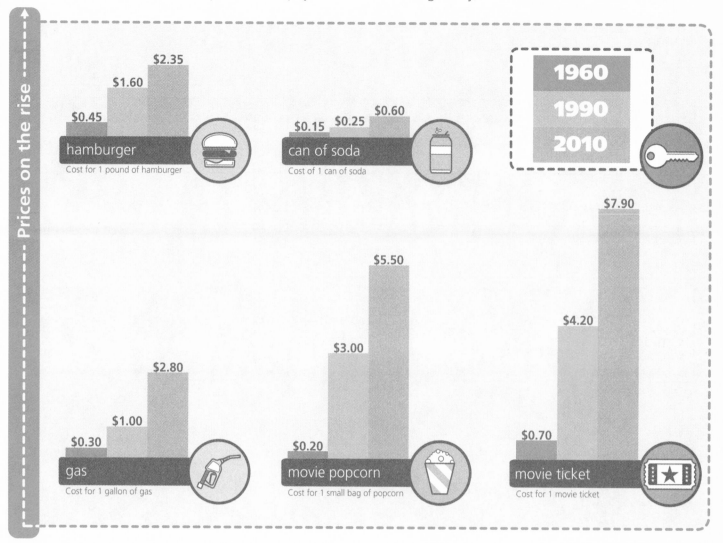

Prices on the rise

hamburger — Cost for 1 pound of hamburger: $0.45, $1.60, $2.35

can of soda — Cost of 1 can of soda: $0.15, $0.25, $0.60

1960 / 1990 / 2010

gas — Cost for 1 gallon of gas: $0.30, $1.00, $2.80

movie popcorn — Cost for 1 small bag of popcorn: $0.20, $3.00, $5.50

movie ticket — Cost for 1 movie ticket: $0.70, $4.20, $7.90

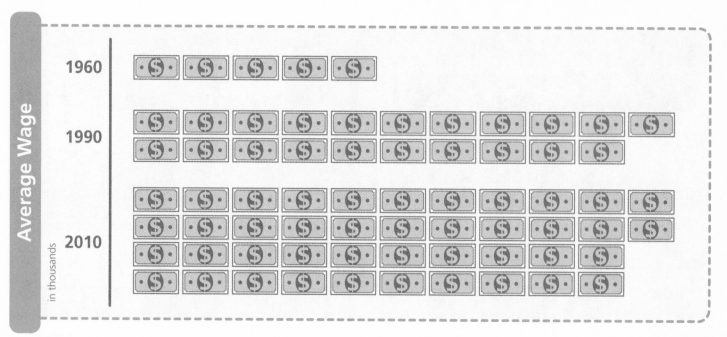

Average Wage (in thousands)

1960
1990
2010

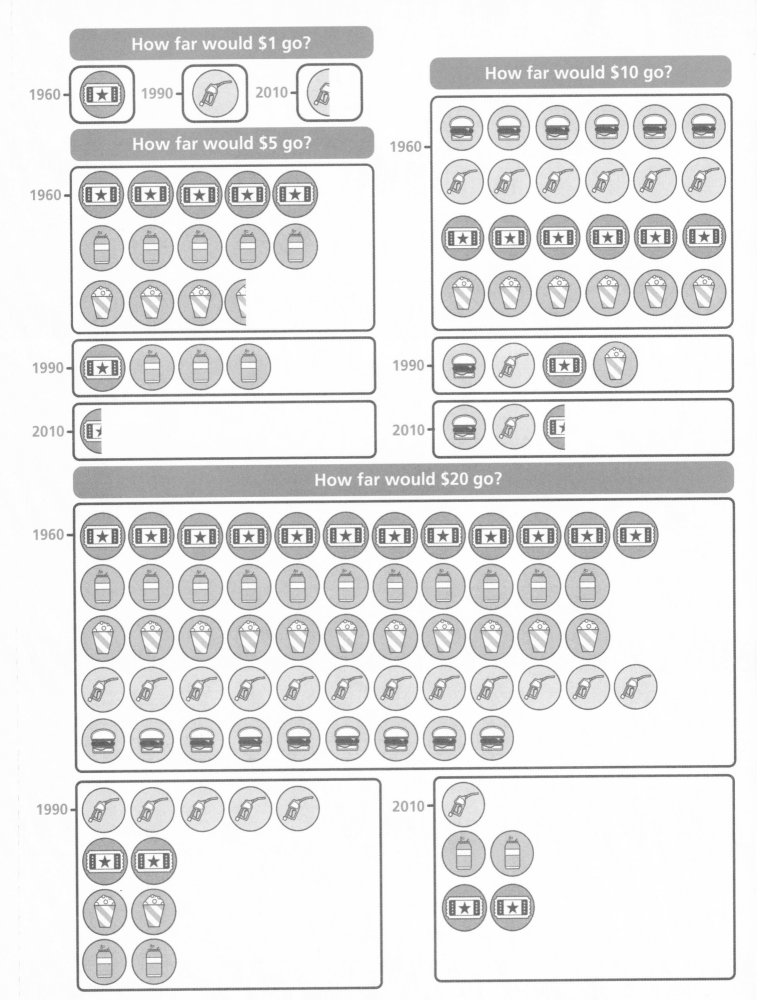

Do the Math

Solve the problems. Use the infographic to help you.

1. In 1960, about how many gallons of gas could you buy for $1?

    A. 1

    B. 3

    C. 5

    D. 7

2. How much more was a gallon of gas in 1990 than in 1960?

_____

3. True or false? A pound of hamburger cost $1.25 in 1990.

_____

4. Which cost more in 1990: two movie tickets or four pounds of hamburger?

_____

5. How much less did a small bag of popcorn cost in 1960 than in 2010?

_____

6. The cost of a gallon of gas _____ from 1990 to 2010.

    A. more than doubled

    B. went up by more than $2.00

    C. stayed the same

    D. fell

7. In 1990, how many movie tickets could you buy for $10.00?

_____

The Visual Guide to Second Grade

Piece It Together

Imagine that you had $100 to spend. What would you buy? Cut apart the items and prices. Then, tape or glue the items you would buy onto page 169. Make sure the items you choose do not add up to more than $100.

video game	baseball cap	science kit	camera	MP3 player

$60	$12	$15	$65	$20

book	comic book	donation to charity	skateboard	art kit

$8	$3	$20	$40	$20

soccer ball	stuffed toy	gift for Mom	gift for Dad	new jeans

$20	$15	$15	$15	$20

yo-yo	jigsaw puzzle	sports team T-shirt	remote-control car	craft kit

$7	$12	$15	$30	$15

savings	trip to the movie theater	board game	ant farm	goldfish and tank
			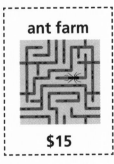	
$20	$15	$13	$15	$30

How Would You Spend $100?

The Space Shuttle

Each orbiter is 122 feet long. That's as long as three school buses!

Each orbiter weighs about 150,000 pounds. That's as much as three train cars!

The Space Shuttle carried many satellites into space.

1981–2011
The Space Shuttle Program

The Space Shuttle sent astronauts into space for 30 years. Before the Space Shuttle, a spacecraft could be used only one time. The Space Shuttle was different. Each orbiter was sent into space using a rocket, but it landed like an airplane. The orbiter could be used again and again.

Each orbiter could carry a crew of up to 7 astronauts.

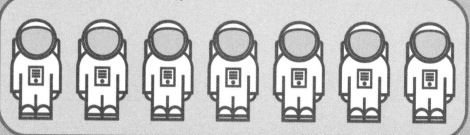

Atlantis

1985–2011	33 Flights

Total miles flown: 126 million

Atlantis was the last Space Shuttle orbiter to go into space. When *Atlantis* landed on July 21, 2011, it marked the end of the Space Shuttle program.

Endeavour

1992–2011	25 Flights

Total miles flown: 123 million

The *Endeavour* was the first orbiter name ever chosen in a national school competition. It was named after a ship that explored the South Pacific Ocean.

Columbia

1981–2003	28 Flights

Total miles flown: 122 million

Sadly, the last flight ended when *Columbia* exploded about 15 minutes before landing.

Challenger

1983–1986	10 Flights

Total miles flown: 24 million

Sadly, the last flight ended when *Challenger* exploded about 1 minute after being launched.

Discovery

1984–2011	39 Flights

Total miles flown: 148 million

The *Discovery* carried the Hubble Space Telescope into orbit in April 1990. Hubble is still in use.

Mae Jemison
- the first African American woman in space
- worked as a doctor before becoming an astronaut
- flew on the *Endeavour* in 1992

Christopher Ferguson
- flew on NASA's last space shuttle, *Atlantis*
- part of a mission that carried astronauts to the International Space Station

Sally Ride
- the first American woman to go into space
- beat 1,000 others to get a spot in NASA's astronaut program
- flew on the *Challenger* in 1983

Carlos Noriega
- went to flight school with the US Marine Corp
- flew on *Atlantis* to help build the International Space Station

Think and Solve

Study the infographic. Answer the questions.

1. _____ was the first American woman to go into space.

2. Why was the Space Shuttle different from spacecraft that came before it?

   A. It was not launched using a rocket.

   B. It was used to orbit the moon.

   C. It could carry people into space.

   D. It could be reused.

3. How many more miles did *Discovery* fly than *Atlantis*?

   _____

Puzzle It

Find and circle each Space Shuttle orbiter name in the puzzle.

```
g  t  i  d  w  z  a  f  g  i  c
j  h  s  y  y  l  n  d  l  u  o
c  h  a  l  l  e  n  g  e  r  l
h  e  t  o  o  n  w  h  p  n  u
o  r  l  p  k  d  e  i  q  y  m
o  a  a  x  b  e  o  i  d  t  b
q  k  n  w  f  a  v  l  a  q  i
v  x  t  j  u  v  s  d  k  r  a
m  d  i  s  c  o  v  e  r  y  l
z  t  s  f  e  u  z  s  p  n  k
y  u  j  u  q  r  d  x  s  x  e
```

Classify It

Read each fact. Circle *T* if it is true and *F* if it is false.

1. **T   F**   *Discovery* was the last Space Shuttle to go into space.

2. **T   F**   *Columbia* and *Challenger* both exploded.

3. **T   F**   The Space Shuttle program ended in 2000.

4. **T   F**   *Discovery* flew more miles than any other Space Shuttle.

5. **T   F**   *Endeavour's* name was chosen in a school competition.

 ## Make a Bar Graph

Use the infographic to help you fill in the bar graph. Beside each orbiter name, draw a bar that shows how long the shuttle flew. Color each bar a different color.

Life of the Space Shuttle Orbiters

Atlantis	
Endeavour	
Discovery	
Columbia	
Challenger	

1980 1982 1984 1986 1988 1990 1992 1994 1996 1998 2000 2002 2004 2006 2008 2010 2012

Leading the Way to Freedom

Harriet Tubman was a conductor on the Underground Railroad who helped people escape from slavery. The "railroad" was a chain of safe places and kind people who offered protection to slaves as they journeyed to freedom in the North. Tubman risked danger by hiding slaves, giving them food and shelter, and telling them where to go next. She will always be remembered for her bravery.

Harriet Tubman was born as Araminta Ross. She changed her name to Harriet after her mother.

She worked on farms as a slave until she was almost 30 years old.

Harriet was well-known by slave hunters. These men tried to capture runaway slaves. They offered large rewards to anyone who could catch Harriet.

"I was the conductor of the Underground Railroad for eight years, and I can say what most conductors can't say — I never ran my train off the track and I never lost a passenger."

– Harriet Tubman

For 10 years, Harriet made secret trips to Maryland and helped slaves escape. She led hundreds of slaves to freedom.

Abolitionists were people who were against slavery. Harriet spoke at their meetings to raise money. Harriet spoke at meetings for women's rights as well. At the time, women were not allowed to vote.

Rights for Women

Harriet was part of the North's Union Army during the Civil War. She was a nurse and a cook.

Harriet and her husband adopted a daughter, Gertie, after the Civil War.

Harriet had a head injury from being mistreated as a slave. She had headaches and seizures the rest of her life.

Harriet Tubman was born in Maryland around 1820. Maryland was a slave state.

She married John Tubman. He was a free black man, but Harriet was still a slave.

1820 **1844**

Harriet escaped to the free state of Pennsylvania. People working for the Underground Railroad helped her make the journey.

Harriet began work as a conductor on the Underground Railroad.

1850 **1849**

After slavery ended, Harriet kept working to help people. In 1896, she worked toward opening a home where poor black families could live.

Harriet Tubman died in 1913.

1896 **1913**

Think and Solve

Study the infographic. Answer the questions.

1. True or false? Both Harriet and John Tubman were slaves.

_____

2. How old was Harriet when she married John?

_____

3. An abolitionist is _____.

    A. someone who is against slavery

    B. a slave who works on a farm

    C. a slave hunter

    D. someone who believes women should have the right to vote

Read About It: What Harriet Said

A *quotation*, or quote, tells exactly what someone said.

Read the quotes below by Harriet Tubman.

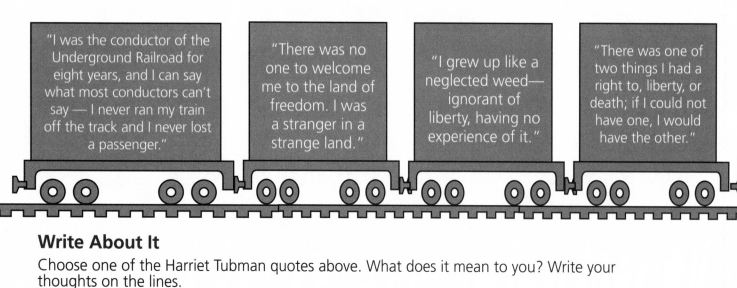

"I was the conductor of the Underground Railroad for eight years, and I can say what most conductors can't say — I never ran my train off the track and I never lost a passenger."

"There was no one to welcome me to the land of freedom. I was a stranger in a strange land."

"I grew up like a neglected weed— ignorant of liberty, having no experience of it."

"There was one of two things I had a right to, liberty, or death; if I could not have one, I would have the other."

Write About It

Choose one of the Harriet Tubman quotes above. What does it mean to you? Write your thoughts on the lines.

_____

_____

_____

_____

Sequence It

Imagine that a cousin sent you the note below giving instructions for using the Underground Railroad. Read the note. Then, number the steps below in the correct order.

Cousin,

Here is what you must to do to find your way to freedom. Save food in the days before you leave. Apples, hard-cooked eggs, bread—anything that will travel well. Wait for a moonless night. Walk through Briar's Creek for as long as you can. If there are dogs, they will not be able to track your scent.

Head north to Wickets' farm. If there is a red shirt on the line, you can stay in the barn during the day. They will leave food for you in the last stall. Keep heading north and travel only at night. Use the North Star to guide your way. You will come to a large wood. The trees will hide you during the day. When you reach the swamp, go around it. Too many dangers lie within. At the other side of the woods, you'll find a small cabin. When two candles flicker in the window, it is safe. Go around back, and you'll be told where to head next.

You must commit this all to memory right away. Then destroy the note. It is not safe for you to keep.

Good luck in your journey.

Cousin Elijah

_____ Head north to Wickets' farm.

_____ Look for a small cabin with two candles in the window.

_____ Walk through Briar's Creek.

_____ Save food in the days before you leave.

_____ Stay in the Wickets' barn during the day.

_____ Go around the swamp.

Answer Key

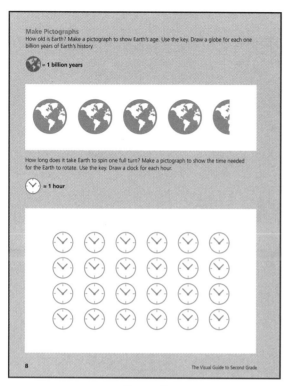

Page 8

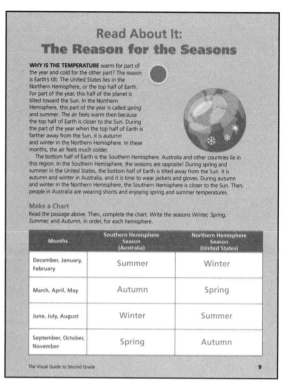

Page 9

Page 12

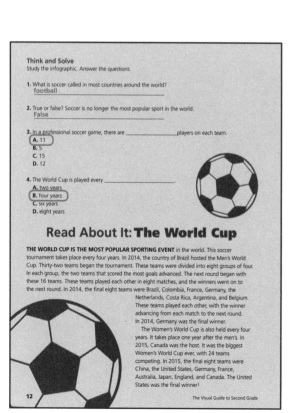

Page 15

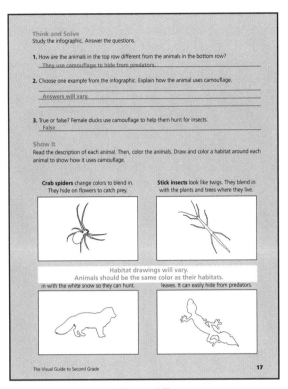

Page 17

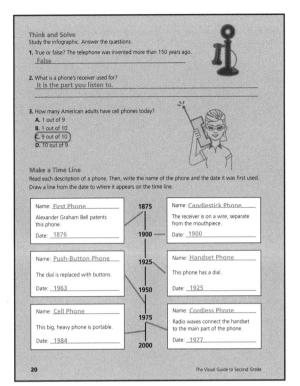

Page 20

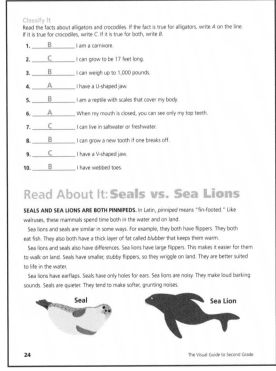

Page 24

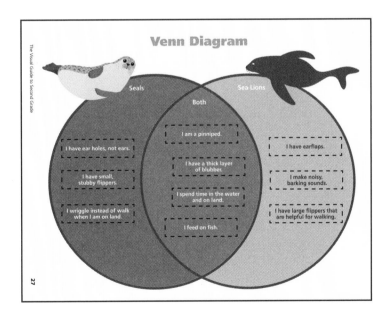

Page 27

Page 29

Think and Solve
Study the infographic. Answer the questions.

1. Ice pops were invented in _____
   - **A.** 1895
   - **B.** 1905
   - **C.** 1915
   - **D.** 1925

2. True or false? In England, ice pops are called *ice lollies*.
   True

3. In the pictograph, each small ice pop is equal to _____ ice pops sold in a year.
   - **A.** 1 million
   - **B.** 5 million
   - **C.** 1 billion
   - **D.** 2 billion

Make a Pictograph
Which flavors of ice pops do kids like best? Conduct a survey to find out. Ask at least 10 students what their favorite flavors are. Draw one ice pop for each answer. 🧊 = one student

Flavor	Students Who Like the Flavor Best
Cherry	
Orange	
Lemon-Lime	Graphs will vary.
Grape	
Strawberry	
Other	

Page 29

Page 35

Think and Solve
Study the infographic. Answer the questions.

1. True or false? A blizzard happens when more than 12 inches of snow fall in an hour.
   False

2. All ice crystals have _____ sides.
   - **A.** 2
   - **B.** 4
   - **C.** 6
   - **D.** 8

3. What color is snow?
   It has no color. It is translucent.

4. If Wisconsin receives 46 inches of snow in a single day, where would it belong in the bar graph?
   between _____ South Dakota _____ and _____ New York _____

Do the Math
Solve the problems. Use the infographic to help you.

1. How much more snow did Colorado receive than New Hampshire?
   22 inches

2. How many feet of snow did Montana receive? (Hint: 1 foot = 12 inches)
   4 feet

3. 60 inches of snow will melt to _____ 6 _____ inches of water.

4. If Tennessee received half the amount of snow that Pennsylvania did, how much did Tennessee receive?
   19 inches

5. How much snow did Colorado, Alaska, and California receive in total?
   185 inches

Page 35

Page 38

Think and Solve
Study the infographic. Answer the questions.

1. The didgeridoo comes from _____
   - **A.** Mexico
   - **B.** Australia
   - **C.** Peru
   - **D.** Japan

2. Choose two instruments. Tell one way they are alike and one way they are different.
   Answers will vary.

3. True or false? When playing the zampoña, the shorter tubes make lower notes.
   False

4. If you could learn to play one of these instruments, which one would you choose? Why?
   Answers will vary.

Read About It: In the Orchestra

AN ORCHESTRA IS A GROUP of many musicians who play together. It is led by a conductor. The orchestra is divided into sections. Each section includes musicians who play similar instruments. There are four main sections. The first section is *strings*. String instruments, such as violins and cellos, make sound when long strings are plucked or played with a bow. The next section is *percussion*. Percussion instruments, such as drums and tambourines, are struck or shaken. The *woodwind* section contains instruments such as flutes that are played by blowing air through long, hollow tubes. The last section is *brass*. Brass instruments are made of metal. To play them, the musician blows air through a tube to make sound.

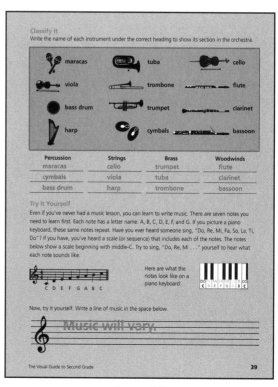

Page 38

Page 39

Classify It
Write the name of each instrument under the correct heading to show its section in the orchestra.

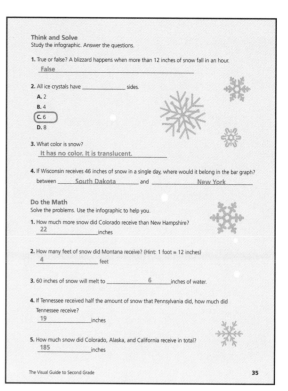

Percussion	Strings	Brass	Woodwinds
maracas	cello	trumpet	flute
cymbals	viola	tuba	clarinet
bass drum	harp	trombone	bassoon

Try It Yourself
Even if you've never had a music lesson, you can learn to write music. There are seven notes you need to learn first. Each note has a letter name: A, B, C, D, E, F, and G. If you picture a piano keyboard, these same notes repeat. Have you ever heard someone sing, "Do, Re, Mi, Fa, So, La, Ti, Do"? If you have, you've heard a scale (or sequence) that includes each of the notes. The notes below show a scale beginning with middle-C. Try to sing, "Do, Re, Mi . . ." yourself to hear what each note sounds like.

Here are what the notes look like on a piano keyboard:

C D E F G A B C

Now, try it yourself. Write a line of music in the space below.

Music will vary.

Page 39

Page 41

Think and Solve
Study the infographic. Answer the questions.

1. True or false? Three teaspoons of sugar equal 12 grams of sugar. _____
  True

2. Young kids should have no more than ___4___ teaspoons of added sugar each day.
  How many grams of sugar are in four teaspoons? ___16___

3. How many teaspoons of sugar are in one serving of peanut butter and one banana?
  A. 5 teaspoons
  B. 7 teaspoons
  C. 12 teaspoons
  D. 15 teaspoons

4. How much more sugar does lemonade have than strawberry yogurt?
  one gram

Log It
Use the chart below to keep track of how many grams of sugar you eat in one day. List each food you eat and the number of grams of sugar it contains.

The amount of sugar in common foods is listed below. If the food you eat is not listed, check the infographic or the label on the package.

small apple = 11 g
clementine = 7 g
1 c strawberries = 7 g
baby carrots = $\frac{1}{2}$ g
cherry tomatoes ($\frac{1}{2}$ c) = 2 g
red potatoes ($\frac{1}{2}$ c) = 1 g
chicken breast = 0 g
beef hamburger = 0 g
beans ($\frac{1}{2}$ c) = 2 g
1 T honey = 17 g
granola bar = 12 g
bagel = 1 g
cornflakes = 2 g
vanilla ice cream = 28 g
milk (1 c) = 13 g

Key:
c = cup   g = gram   T = tablespoon

Food	Grams of Sugar

Logs will vary.

Do you think you eat too much sugar? Why or why not?

_____
_____

Page 41

Page 44

Think and Solve
Study the infographic. Answer the questions.

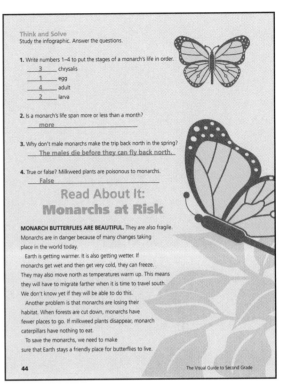

1. Write numbers 1–4 to put the stages of a monarch's life in order.
  ___3___ chrysalis
  ___1___ egg
  ___4___ adult
  ___2___ larva

2. Is a monarch's life span more or less than a month?
  more

3. Why don't male monarchs make the trip back north in the spring?
  The males die before they can fly back north.

4. True or false? Milkweed plants are poisonous to monarchs.
  False

Read About It:
Monarchs at Risk

MONARCH BUTTERFLIES ARE BEAUTIFUL. They are also fragile. Monarchs are in danger because of many changes taking place in the world today.

Earth is getting warmer. It is also getting wetter. If monarchs get wet and then get very cold, they can freeze. They may also move north as temperatures warm up. This means they will have to migrate farther when it is time to travel south. We don't know yet if they will be able to do this.

Another problem is that monarchs are losing their habitat. When forests are cut down, monarchs have fewer places to go. If milkweed plants disappear, monarch caterpillars have nothing to eat.

To save the monarchs, we need to make sure that Earth stays a friendly place for butterflies to live.

Page 44

Page 48

Think and Solve
Study the infographic. Answer the questions.

1. Silk was invented about ___700___ years before pasta.

2. Which is the newest invention shown on the infographic?
  A. gunpowder
  B. silk
  C. paper
  D. wheelbarrow

3. List the three cities shown on the map of China. Circle the name of the capital city.
  Beijing
  Shanghai
  Hong Kong

4. True or false? Paper was invented before kites.
  False

5. Which invention do you think was the most important? Why?
  _____
  Answers will vary.
  _____

6. True or false? The radio was invented in Ancient China.
  False

Page 48

Page 51

Think and Solve
Study the infographic. Answer the questions.

1. What fraction of an iceberg is under water? $\frac{9}{10}$
  _____

2. True or false? Icebergs are frozen chunks of salt water floating in the ocean.
  False

3. Why are small icebergs sometimes more dangerous than large ones?
  They are harder to see in the water.

4. Icebergs are found _____
  A. only at the North Pole
  B. only at the South Pole
  C. only in Iceberg Alley
  D. in the oceans near both poles

Try It Yourself
Icebergs float because ice is less dense (heavy) than liquid water. Try this experiment to prove it.

Materials:
- a clear cup
- food coloring
- baby oil
- vegetable oil
- an ice cube

Procedure:
1. Place a few of drops of food coloring in the cup.
2. Fill it halfway with vegetable oil. Fill it the rest of the way with baby oil.
3. Now, add the ice cube. It will float in the middle of the cup.
4. Be patient and watch. After a little while, the ice cube will start to melt.
5. The drops of water from the ice cube will sink to the bottom and mix with the food coloring.
6. The ice cube will keep floating. That's because ice is less dense than water!

Page 51

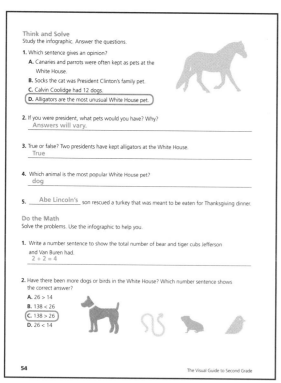

Page 54

Think and Solve
Study the infographic. Answer the questions.

1. Which sentence gives an opinion?
   A. Canaries and parrots were often kept as pets at the White House.
   B. Socks the cat was President Clinton's family pet.
   C. Calvin Coolidge had 12 dogs.
   D. Alligators are the most unusual White House pet.

2. If you were president, what pets would you have? Why?
   Answers will vary.

3. True or false? Two presidents have kept alligators at the White House.
   True

4. Which animal is the most popular White House pet?
   dog

5. _Abe Lincoln's_ son rescued a turkey that was meant to be eaten for Thanksgiving dinner.

Do the Math
Solve the problems. Use the infographic to help you.

1. Write a number sentence to show the total number of bear and tiger cubs Jefferson and Van Buren had.
   2 + 2 = 4

2. Have there been more dogs or birds in the White House? Which number sentence shows the correct answer?
   A. 26 > 14
   B. 138 < 26
   C. 138 > 26
   D. 26 < 14

54   The Visual Guide to Second Grade

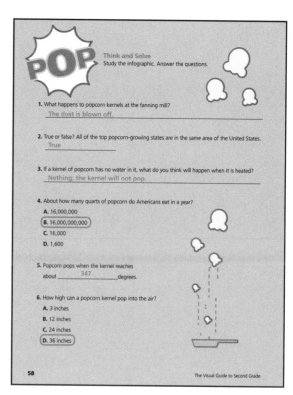

Page 58

POP

Think and Solve
Study the infographic. Answer the questions.

1. What happens to popcorn kernels at the fanning mill?
   The dust is blown off.

2. True or false? All of the top popcorn-growing states are in the same area of the United States.
   True

3. If a kernel of popcorn has no water in it, what do you think will happen when it is heated?
   Nothing; the kernel will not pop.

4. About how many quarts of popcorn do Americans eat in a year?
   A. 16,000,000
   B. 16,000,000,000
   C. 16,000
   D. 1,600

5. Popcorn pops when the kernel reaches about _____347_____ degrees.

6. How high can a popcorn kernel pop into the air?
   A. 3 inches
   B. 12 inches
   C. 24 inches
   D. 36 inches

58   The Visual Guide to Second Grade

Page 63

Olympic Events

Winter Olympics

figure skating   snowboarding   luge   hockey

skiing   bobsled   speed skating   ski jumping

Summer Olympics

volleyball   soccer   swimming   fencing

gymnastics   equestrian   basketball   cycling

The Visual Guide to Second Grade   63

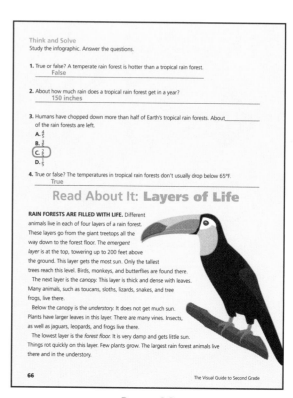

Page 66

Think and Solve
Study the infographic. Answer the questions.

1. True or false? A temperate rain forest is hotter than a tropical rain forest.
   False

2. About how much rain does a tropical rain forest get in a year?
   150 inches

3. Humans have chopped down more than half of Earth's tropical rain forests. About_____ of the rain forests are left.
   A. $\frac{4}{5}$
   B. $\frac{3}{4}$
   C. $\frac{2}{5}$
   D. $\frac{1}{5}$

4. True or false? The temperatures in tropical rain forests don't usually drop below 65°F.
   True

Read About It: Layers of Life

RAIN FORESTS ARE FILLED WITH LIFE. Different animals live in each of four layers of a rain forest. These layers go from the giant treetops all the way down to the forest floor. The _emergent layer_ is at the top, towering up to 200 feet above the ground. This layer gets the most sun. Only the tallest trees reach this level. Birds, monkeys, and butterflies are found there.

The next layer is the _canopy._ This layer is thick and dense with leaves. Many animals, such as toucans, sloths, lizards, snakes, and tree frogs, live there.

Below the canopy is the _understory._ It does not get much sun. Plants have larger leaves in this layer. There are many vines. Insects, as well as jaguars, leopards, and frogs live there.

The lowest layer is the _forest floor._ It is very damp and gets little sun. Things rot quickly on this layer. Few plants grow. The largest rain forest animals live there and in the understory.

66   The Visual Guide to Second Grade

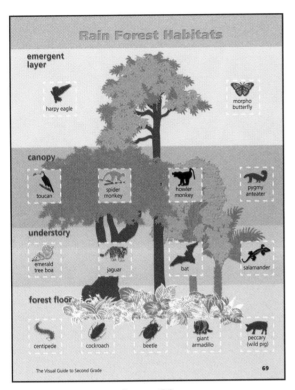

Page 69

Rain Forest Habitats

emergent layer
- harpy eagle
- morpho butterfly

canopy
- toucan
- spider monkey
- howler monkey
- pygmy anteater

understory
- emerald tree boa
- jaguar
- bat
- salamander

forest floor
- centipede
- cockroach
- beetle
- giant armadillo
- peccary (wild pig)

The Visual Guide to Second Grade
69

Page 71

Think and Solve
Study the infographic. Answer the questions.

1. Why does a firefighter carry an axe?
to break down doors, windows, walls, or roofs

2. True or false? A firefighter's gear weighs more than 100 pounds.
False

3. Read each sentence. Write *F* if the sentence tells a fact. Write *O* if it tells an opinion.
- F — A firefighter's hat costs about $200.
- O — The most important piece of equipment is the air tank.
- O — Hiking boots are more comfortable than steel-toe boots.
- F — Thick, padded gloves protect a firefighter's hands.

4. Write the names of two other pieces of firefighting equipment not shown in the infographic.
Possible answers: hose and fire truck

5. What is special about the fabric used to make a turnout coat and pants?
A. It is very light.
B. It is waterproof and heatproof.
C. It is made of rubber.
D. It glows in the dark.

Classify It
These words and phrases relate to firefighting. Write *N* beside each noun (naming word).
Write *V* beside each verb (action word). Write *A* beside each adjective (describing word).

A hot	A expensive	N smoke	N debris
N fire	V to break	V to breathe	N victims
V to fight	N roof	V to spray	N mask
A safe	A reflective	V to protect	A thick
A padded	A waterproof	A heavy	V to help

The Visual Guide to Second Grade
71

Page 74

Think and Solve
Study the infographic. Answer the questions.

1. Where is the tallest waterfall in North America?
Yosemite National Park

2. True or false? The tallest mountain in the United States is Cadillac Mountain in Acadia National Park.
False

3. Crater Lake is the _____ lake in the United States.
A. biggest
B. oldest
C. deepest
D. coldest

4. Which park is the largest National Park shown in the infographic?
Yellowstone National Park

Make a Time Line
Make a time line to show when National Parks were established (founded). Write the names of the parks in the spaces on the time line. Use the infographic to help you.

1870 — Yellowstone
1880
— Yosemite
1890 — Mount Rainier
1900
— Crater Lake
1910 — Glacier
— Acadia
1920 — Rocky Mountain
— Hot Springs
1930
— Shenandoah
1940 — Everglades
— Mammoth Cave
1950

74
The Visual Guide to Second Grade

Page 75

Make a Chart
Complete the chart. List the five parks from the infographic that had the most visitors in 2014.

National Parks with the Most Visitors, 2014

Rank	Park Name	Number of Visitors
1st	Yosemite	3,882,642
2nd	Yellowstone	3,513,484
3rd	Rocky Mountain	3,434,751
4th	Acadia	2,563,129
5th	Glacier	2,338,528

Schedule It
Imagine you have one week to visit three National Parks. Which ones will you choose to see? How many days will you stay at each park? Remember, you will need to drive from one park to the next. Choose parks that are near each other. Fill in the calendar to plan your week.

Sunday	Monday	Tuesday	Wednesday	Thursday	Friday	Saturday

Calendars will vary.

Which park would you most like to visit? Why?

Responses will vary.

The Visual Guide to Second Grade
75

Page 78

Think and Solve
Study the infographic. Answer the questions.

1. True or false? A sound that is 4,000 Hz is always louder than a sound that is 60 Hz.

False

2. Sounds above _____ dB can cause pain.
A. 60
B. 85
C. 100
D. 120 ⟵ (circled)

3. A truck goes by. The sound it makes has a pitch of 50 Hz. What does this information tell you?
A. The truck made a high sound.
B. The truck made a low sound. ⟵ (circled)
C. The truck is loud.
D. The truck is quiet.

4. A radio is turned up to 75 dB. Describe where you would place the radio in the infographic.

on the loudness graph, between the people talking and the lawnmower

5. A dog whistle makes a sound at 30,000 Hz. What does this tell you about dogs?

Dogs can hear higher sounds than humans.

6. Smaller waves go together with (quieter, louder) sounds.

quieter

7. Explain how hearing works.

Sound waves enter the ear, make the eardrum move, and the brain reads

the vibrations.

Page 78

Page 83

Venn Diagram

President Theodore Roosevelt

President John F. Kennedy

Both

Theodore Roosevelt was the 26th president.

Roosevelt became president after President McKinley was shot.

Roosevelt loved nature and worked to protect the nation's forests.

Roosevelt was a Republican.

When elected, Kennedy and Roosevelt were both the country's youngest president.

Kennedy and Roosevelt both went to Harvard.

Kennedy and Roosevelt both fought in wars.

Kennedy and Roosevelt were both born into wealthy families.

Kennedy was a Democrat.

John F. Kennedy was the 35th president.

Kennedy was assassinated while in office.

Kennedy created the Peace Corps to help people in struggling nations.

Page 83

Page 86

Think and Solve
Study the infographic. Answer the questions.

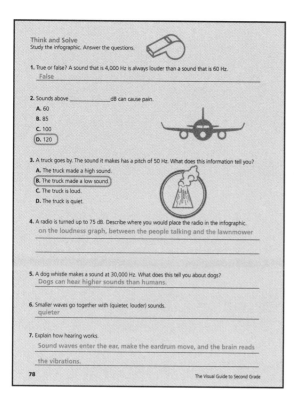

1. True or false? _Magma_ and _lava_ both mean "molten rock."

True

2. Which volcano is the most active?
A. Mauna Loa ⟵ (circled)
B. Mt. Vesuvius
C. Mt. St. Helens
D. Krakatoa

3. How many volcanoes shown in the infographic are in the United States?

two

4. What is a tsunami?
A. an earthquake caused by a volcano
B. a volcano that oozes lava steadily
C. a giant wave ⟵ (circled)
D. another name for magma

Classify It
Use the infographic. Write the name of each volcano under the name of the continent where it is found. Hint: You will not use every line.

Africa	Asia	North America	South America	Australia	Europe
	Mt. Pinatubo	Mauna Loa			Eyjafjallajökull
	Krakatoa	Mount St. Helens			Mt. Vesuvius
	Mt. Tambora	Mt. Pelée			

Page 86

Page 87

Match It
Draw a line to match each fact with the name of the volcano it describes.

erupted above St. Pierre
almost 14,000 feet tall
one of the biggest eruptions ever recorded
erupted in 2010
its eruption was many times stronger than an atom bomb
destroyed Pompeii 2,000 years ago
erupted in 1991 and affected temperatures for two years
shot ash and stone at speeds of 300 miles per hour

Mt. Tambora
Mt. Vesuvius
Mt. Pinatubo
Mauna Loa
Krakatoa
Mt. Pelée
Mt. St. Helens
Eyjafjallajökull

Try It Yourself
Make your own volcano! With an adult's help, follow the steps below. Be sure to make your volcano in a place that can get messy.

What you need:
• clay
• a small container, such as a yogurt cup
• tablespoon
• baking soda
• dish soap
• red and yellow food coloring
• vinegar

What you do:
1. Use the clay to form a mountain with the container in the middle. Be sure the container is open at the top.

2. Pour **two tablespoons of baking soda** into the container.

3. Pour **one tablespoon of dish soap** into the container.

4. Add **four drops of red food coloring** and **four drops of yellow food coloring**.

5. Add **two tablespoons of vinegar** and watch out!

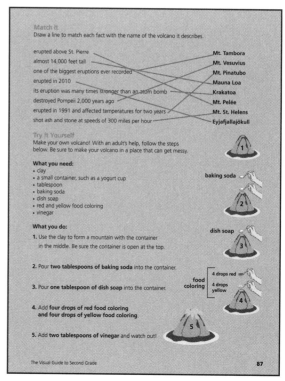

baking soda

dish soap

food coloring — 4 drops red / 4 drops yellow

Page 87

Page 89

Read About It: Ellis Island

ELLIS ISLAND IS A SMALL ISLAND in New York. In 1892, it opened as an immigration station. People came from other countries by boat. At Ellis Island, they learned if they could stay in America. They had to show that they were healthy. They answered many questions. Could they read and write? Did they have family in the US? Did they have any money? Did they speak English? Those who passed the test were allowed into the country. Others had to wait. Some were sent back home. Today, about four out of every ten Americans have a relative who passed through Ellis Island!

The first immigrants came through Ellis Island in **1892**. There were about 450,000 that year. For the next ten years, the numbers were steady: **1893** (350,000), **1894** (200,000), **1895** (200,000), **1896** (250,000), **1897** (200,000), **1898** (200,000), **1899** (250,000), **1900** (350,000), **1901** (400,000), **1902** (500,000). The numbers grew even higher in the years right before World War I.

Think and Solve
Study the infographic and the passage above. Answer the questions.

1. True or false? The Statue of Liberty was a gift to America from the people of England.

False

2. Brooklyn is _____ of the Statue of Liberty.
   A. north
   B. east
   C. south
   D. west

3. Because the statue is made of ___copper___, it turned from brown to green.

4. How did people arrive at Ellis Island?

by boat

5. True or false? More people wanted to come to the US right before World War I began.

True

Page 89

Page 90

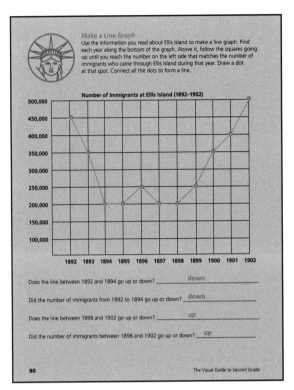

Make a Line Graph
Use the information you read about Ellis Island to make a line graph. Find each year along the bottom of the graph. Above it, follow the squares going up until you reach the number on the left side that matches the number of immigrants who came through Ellis Island during that year. Draw a dot at that spot. Connect all the dots to form a line.

Number of Immigrants at Ellis Island (1892–1902)

Does the line between 1892 and 1894 go up or down? ___down___

Did the number of immigrants from 1892 to 1894 go up or down? ___down___

Does the line between 1898 and 1902 go up or down? ___up___

Did the number of immigrants between 1898 and 1902 go up or down? ___up___

Page 90

Page 94

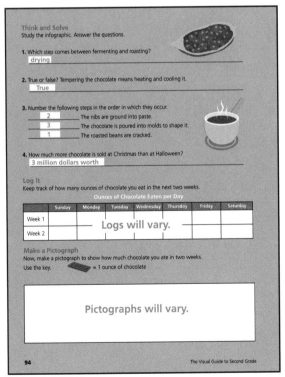

Think and Solve
Study the infographic. Answer the questions.

1. Which step comes between fermenting and roasting?
drying

2. True or false? Tempering the chocolate means heating and cooling it.
True

3. Number the following steps in the order in which they occur.
   _2_ The nibs are ground into paste.
   _3_ The chocolate is poured into molds to shape it.
   _1_ The roasted beans are cracked.

4. How much more chocolate is sold at Christmas than at Halloween?
3 million dollars worth

Log It
Keep track of how many ounces of chocolate you eat in the next two weeks.

Ounces of Chocolate Eaten per Day

	Sunday	Monday	Tuesday	Wednesday	Thursday	Friday	Saturday
Week 1							
Week 2		Logs will vary.					

Make a Pictograph
Now, make a pictograph to show how much chocolate you ate in two weeks.
Use the key. ▬ = 1 ounce of chocolate

Pictographs will vary.

Page 94

Page 98

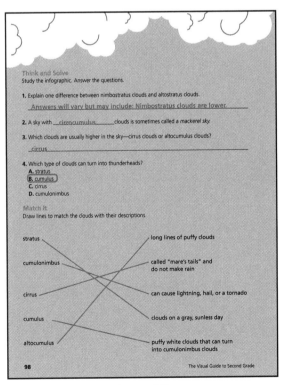

Think and Solve
Study the infographic. Answer the questions.

1. Explain one difference between nimbostratus clouds and altostratus clouds.
Answers will vary but may include: Nimbostratus clouds are lower.

2. A sky with ___cirrocumulus___ clouds is sometimes called a *mackerel sky*.

3. Which clouds are usually higher in the sky—cirrus clouds or altocumulus clouds?
cirrus

4. Which type of clouds can turn into thunderheads?
   A. stratus
   B. cumulus
   C. cirrus
   D. cumulonimbus

Match It
Draw lines to match the clouds with their descriptions.

stratus   long lines of puffy clouds

cumulonimbus   called "mare's tails" and do not make rain

cirrus   can cause lightning, hail, or a tornado

cumulus   clouds on a gray, sunless day

altocumulus   puffy white clouds that can turn into cumulonimbus clouds

Page 98

Page 106

Study the infographic. Answer the questions.

1. True or false? A balloon filled with hot air is denser than a balloon filled with cold air.

False

2. The highest a balloon flew carrying a person was more than _____ miles.

(A.) 21
B. 35
C. 72
D. 114

3. When did the first balloon cross the Pacific Ocean?

_1981_

4. Why does a cork float?

because it is less dense than water

Puzzle It
Read each clue below. Fill in the answers to complete the crossword puzzle.

Across

1. A cork will float in _____

5. What is the infographic's main idea? What is it mostly about?

6. What animal flew with a rooster and a duck on the first balloon flight?

Down

2. Which ocean was crossed in a helium balloon in 1978?

3. A balloon crossed the _____ Channel in 1785.

4. Hydrogen is less _____ than regular air.

Crossword: W A T E R (across), B A L L O O N S, S H E E P. Down: T L N T I C, E N S I S H, D E S S

Page 106

Page 109

Study the infographic. Answer the questions.

1. Read the word. Circle the part of the word that means "light, glow."

bio luminescence

2. What causes some plants and animals to glow?
A. heat
(B. chemical reactions)
C. reflecting sunlight
D. reflecting moonlight

3. True or false? Fireflies glow to help them hunt for food at night.

False

4. Number the animals from smallest to largest.

_2_ firefly _3_ anglerfish _1_ dinoflagellate

5. Large groups of dinoflagellates are called _blooms_.

Imagine It
Imagine you are a scientist who has discovered a new bioluminescent creature. In the box below, draw what it looks like. Then, write about the creature on the lines below. Where does the animal live? What body parts glow? Why does it glow?

Drawings and descriptions will vary.

Page 109

Page 112

Study the infographic. Answer the questions.

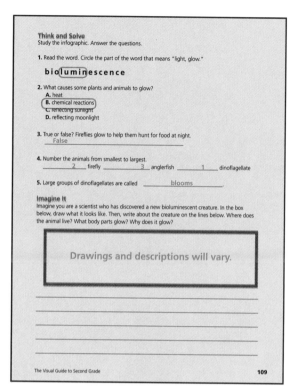

1. Which man never served as president of the United States?
A. Thomas Jefferson
(B. Benjamin Franklin)
C. Andrew Jackson
D. Ulysses S. Grant

2. True or false? Abraham Lincoln was president before Ulysses S. Grant.
True

3. How many old bills were destroyed in 2010?
A. 6,000
B. 6,000,000
(C. 6,000,000,000)
D. 600

4. Who was Sacagawea?
Sacagawea was a Native American woman who traveled with Lewis and Clark.

Do the Math
Javier has six different bills and coins. They total $26.31. Circle the bills and coins that he has.

Page 112

Page 117

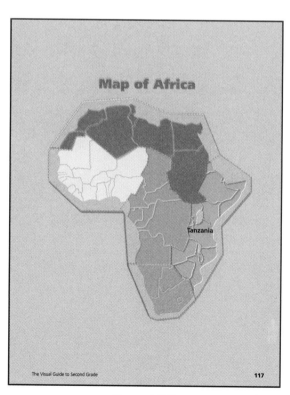

Map of Africa

Tanzania

Page 117

Page 119

Think and Solve
Study the infographic. Answer the questions.

1. Soldiers in World War II got in the habit of brushing their teeth in the army. When they came home, they _____
   A. could not buy toothpaste
   B. brought the habit with them
   C. did not bring their toothbrushes
   D. stopped brushing

2. Before nylon, what were toothbrush bristles made from?
   hog and horse hair

3. The Chinese made chewing sticks from _____ twigs _____

4. True or false? At one point in time, humans used their fingers as toothbrushes.
   True

Log It
Each day, you should brush your teeth at least twice (in the morning and before bed). Each time you brush, you should keep brushing for two whole minutes. Keep track of how long you brush your teeth this week. Each empty hourglass is equal to two minutes of brushing. Color one hourglass for every two minutes you spend brushing.

Logs will vary.

Page 119

Page 120

The chart below shows baby teeth and their names. Read the labels on the right side of the mouth. Use them to help you label the teeth on the left side.

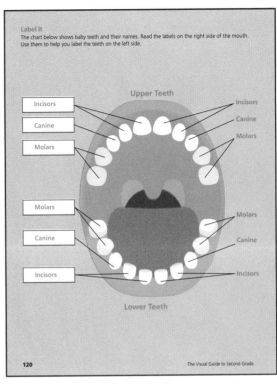

Upper Teeth

Incisors — Incisors
Canine — Canine
Molars — Molars
Molars — Molars
Canine — Canine
Incisors — Incisors

Lower Teeth

Page 120

Page 121

Use the diagram on page 120. Answer the questions.

1. How many baby teeth do humans have?
   _20_

2. True or false? The teeth on the left side of your mouth are the same as on the right side.
   True

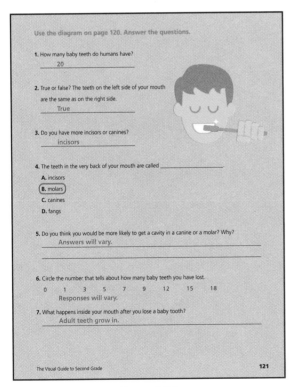

3. Do you have more incisors or canines?
   incisors

4. The teeth in the very back of your mouth are called _____
   A. incisors
   B. molars
   C. canines
   D. fangs

5. Do you think you would be more likely to get a cavity in a canine or a molar? Why?
   Answers will vary.

6. Circle the number that tells about how many baby teeth you have lost.
   0   1   3   5   7   9   12   15   18
   Responses will vary.

7. What happens inside your mouth after you lose a baby tooth?
   Adult teeth grow in.

Page 121

Page 124

Think and Solve
Study the infographic. Answer the questions.

1. Alaska and Hawaii were the last two states to join the union. Did they become states before or after 1959? How do you know?
   after; until 1959, the flag had 48 stars

2. How many more stars did the 1863 flag have than the 1822 flag?
   _11_

3. Draw a line to match each color to what it symbolizes on the flag.
   red — caution, hard work, and fairness
   white — strength and bravery
   blue — honesty and innocence

4. Which is not a nickname for the American flag?
   A. the Stars and Stripes
   B. the Star-Spangled Banner
   C. Starry Night
   D. Old Glory

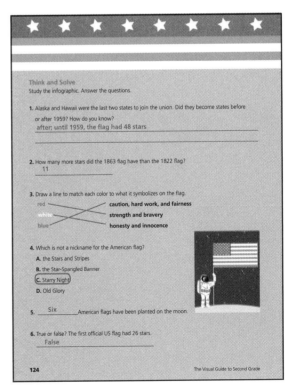

5. _Six_ American flags have been planted on the moon.

6. True or false? The first official US flag had 26 stars.
   False

Page 124

Page 125

This US map shows the date that each state became a part of the country. Look at the map. In the stars below, write the abbreviations for the first 13 states to become part of the United States of America. They should be in order by the date they joined the union.

Stars (in order):
DE, PA, NJ, GA, CT
MA, MD, SC, NH, VA
NY, NC, RI

The Visual Guide to Second Grade   125

Page 127

Think and Solve
Study the infographic. Answer the questions.

1. True or false? There are no land mammals living in Antarctica.
_____True_____

2. The __Arctic__ Ocean is below the ice sheet that covers the Arctic.

3. Robert Peary reached the __North__ Pole in 1909.

4. Which is colder, the Arctic or Antarctica?
_____Antarctica_____

Compare and Contrast
Read the facts. If a fact tells only about the Arctic, write it in the left circle. If a fact tells only about Antarctica, write it in the right circle. If the fact tells about both places, write it in the middle.

polar bears live there   countries have land there   no countries have land there

covered in an ice sheet   land beneath the ice sheet   where the North Pole is

people live there   where the South Pole is   whales live there

Venn diagram:
- NP / The Arctic (left): polar bears live there, countries have land there, where the North Pole is
- Both Places (middle): covered in an ice sheet, people live there, whales live there
- Antarctica / SP (right): no countries have land there, land beneath the ice sheet, where the South Pole is

---

Page 130

Think and Solve
Study the infographic. Answer the questions.

1. True or false? Only Number 1 plastic can be recycled.
__False__

2. A store sells 5,000 water bottles in one month. How many of those water bottles can be recycled?
__5,000__

About how many of the water bottles will be recycled?
__1,000__

About how many will be buried in a landfill?
__4,000__

3. Write 0 on each line below to show the number of water bottles sold each year.
5, _0_ _0_ _0_, _0_ _0_ _0_, _0_ _0_ _0_

4. Most things made of plastic are marked with a number in a triangle. What does the number tell you?
(A. the type of plastic)
B. where the plastic was made
C. how many times the plastic can be recycled
D. all of the above

5. If you drink only tap water for three years, about how much will you spend on drinking water?
A. 50¢
B. $1.25
(C. $1.50)
D. $3.00

130   The Visual Guide to Second Grade

Page 134

Think and Solve
Study the infographic. Answer the questions.

1. True or false? Jackie Robinson won the first MLB Rookie of the Year Award.
__True__

2. What were the Negro Leagues?
__leagues where black people could play baseball professionally__

3. True or false? Jackie Robinson starred in a movie about himself after he retired from baseball.
__False__

4. What is the NAACP?
__National Association for the Advancement of Colored People__

5. Which sport is not listed as one Jackie played?
A. track
B. basketball
C. football
(D. soccer)

6. How old was Jackie when he died?
__53 years old__

7. What do you think it means to "retire" a player's uniform number?
__to decide that no other player can use the number__

134   The Visual Guide to Second Grade

Page 138

1. True or false? Telling and tattling are the same thing.
   False

2. What are three examples of bullying?
   Answers will vary. _____ _____

3. If you are being bullied, the most important thing to do is _____.
   A. ignore it
   B. get revenge
   C. bottle up your feelings
   (D.) tell an adult

Read About It:
Stopping Bullies in the Act
Read each scene. On the lines, write advice you would give to the child who is being bullied.

MAGGIE IS NEW AT SCHOOL. At lunch, she holds her tray and looks for somewhere to sit. She sees some girls from her class. Maggie asks if she can sit with them. One girl, Jaden, smirks at Maggie. "Sorry," she says, in a singsong voice. "These seats are all taken." She turns her back to Maggie and laughs with her friends.

Answers will vary.

Page 138

Page 142

1. Which lake is located west of the Grand Canyon?
   Lake Mead

2. Can ponderosa pines live for longer than one century?
   yes

3. The Grand Canyon is located in _____
   A. Colorado
   B. Utah
   (C.) Arizona
   D. Connecticut

4. Rounded to the nearest ten, the Grand Canyon is _____20_____ miles across at its widest point.

Write About It
Pretend you are visiting the Grand Canyon. On the back of the postcard below, write a note to a friend.

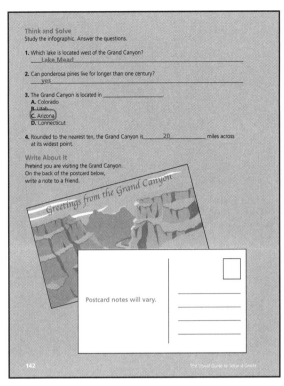

Greetings from the Grand Canyon

Postcard notes will vary.

Page 142

Page 145

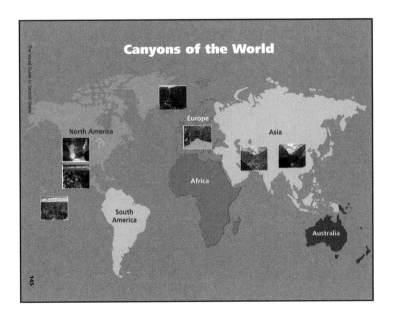

Canyons of the World

North America

Europe

Asia

Africa

South America

Australia

Page 145

Page 148

1. Phillip Hinkle built the first _____
   A. looping roller coaster
   (B.) roller coaster like the ones we see today
   C. steel roller coaster
   D. flume

2. True or false? The Matterhorn was the first looping roller coaster built at Disneyland.
   False

3. Why are there no more roller coasters with loops shaped like circles?
   because oval loops are safer

4. How steep was the Wildcat?
   A. 35 degrees
   B. 45 degrees
   (C.) 60 degrees
   D. 90 degrees

Match It
Draw a line from each coaster on the left to its description on the right.

strata coaster — a roller coaster 300 feet or taller
mega coaster — a roller coaster 150 feet to 220 feet tall
giga coaster — a roller coaster 400 feet or taller
hyper coaster — a ride like a roller coaster, but with boats and water
flume — a roller coaster 200 feet or taller

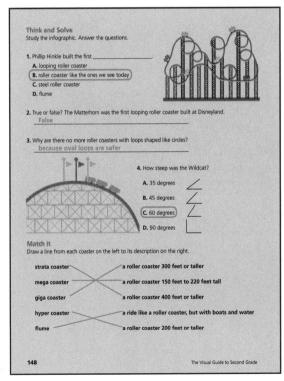

Page 148

Page 151

Think and Solve
Study the infographic. Answer the questions.

1. Which layer is thicker—the crust or the mantle?
   _____the mantle_____

2. True or false? Geologists can't drill deeper than Earth's crust.
   _____True_____

3. The center of Earth is called the _____inner core_____.

4. Earth's inner core is made of _____.
   A. diamonds
   B. iron and nickel
   C. oxygen and nickel
   D. hot lava

Try It Yourself
Make your own three-dimensional model of Earth's layers. Follow the directions.

1. You will need modeling clay in five different colors, including green and blue. You will also need a ruler with centimeter measurements.
2. Make three balls. The first should be about 1 cm across. It will be Earth's inner core.
3. Next, make a ball about 3 cm across for the outer core.
4. Make the third ball about 6 cm across. This is the mantle.
5. Cover the inner core with the outer core.
6. Cover the outer core with the mantle.
7. Last, make a thick layer of blue and green over the mantle. This is Earth's crust.
8. Ask an adult to carefully cut open your Earth to see its layers.

Page 151

Page 154

Do the Math
Solve the problems. Use the infographic to help you.

1. How many feet taller is the tallest mountain ash than the tallest klinki pine?
   _____32_____ feet

2. If the tallest pin oak and the tallest sitka spruce were stacked together, how tall would the stack be?
   _____418_____ feet

3. How many feet taller is the tallest giant sequoia than the tallest sweetgum?
   _____192_____ feet

4. If the tallest pin oak were measured in ten sections, how long would each section be?
   _____10_____ feet

5. How many six-foot people would need to be stacked to match the height of the tallest sitka spruce?
   _____53_____ six-foot people

Explore Your World
Is there a tall tree in your yard, in your neighborhood, or in a nearby park? Did you ever wonder how tall the tree is? Follow these steps to find out.

1. Choose the tree you want to measure.

2. Turn your back to the tree and bend down. Look through your legs at the tree.

3. Move closer or farther away until you can see the tree from top to bottom between your legs.

4. When you have found the right spot, turn around.

5. Mark your spot and measure the distance to the tree in feet. This distance will be about the height of the tree.

Page 154

Page 158

Think and Solve
Study the infographic. Answer the questions.

1. True or false? Teddy Roosevelt was the youngest person to become president.
   _____True_____

2. Roosevelt led soldiers on horseback during _____
   A. the Civil War
   B. the War of 1812
   C. World War I
   D. the Spanish-American War

3. According to the infographic, why was Roosevelt stubborn?
   He was sick and weak as a child. He did not give up. He worked hard to
   become strong and healthy.

4. What kind of building did Roosevelt compare a redwood forest to?
   a cathedral

5. Adjectives are describing words. The infographic lists eight adjectives that describe Teddy Roosevelt. Write one more adjective that describes Roosevelt and tell why you think it is true.
   Answers will vary.

6. Which is not one of Roosevelt's accomplishments?
   A. winning the Nobel Peace Prize
   B. creating the first wildlife refuge in the US
   C. traveling to the North Pole
   D. climbing the Swiss Alps

Page 158

Page 159

Read About It:
Roosevelt's Gifts to the Future

TEDDY ROOSEVELT LOVED THE OUTDOORS. He knew that the US was rich in natural and wild places. He also understood that these special areas needed to be protected. Otherwise, they would not be there in the future. While he was president, Roosevelt set aside 230 million acres of land to be protected.

He created five National Parks. The first was Crater Lake National Park in Oregon in 1902. He also created 18 National Monuments, including Natural Bridges in Utah. Another National Monument he created was the Grand Canyon. Later, it became a National Park.

Forests were protected by Roosevelt as well. He created 150 National Forests! Tongass National Forest in Alaska is the largest National Forest in the US. It was created by Roosevelt in 1907.

Roosevelt loved all wildlife, but birds in particular. He created 51 Bird Reserves during his presidency. These were the first wildlife refuges in the US. Today, there are more than 500!

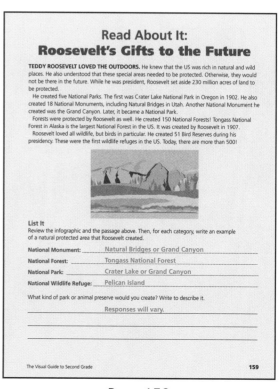

List It
Review the infographic and the passage above. Then, for each category, write an example of a natural protected area that Roosevelt created.

National Monument: _____Natural Bridges or Grand Canyon_____

National Forest: _____Tongass National Forest_____

National Park: _____Crater Lake or Grand Canyon_____

National Wildlife Refuge: _____Pelican Island_____

What kind of park or animal preserve would you create? Write to describe it.
_____Responses will vary._____
_____
_____

Page 159

Page 162

Study the infographic. Answer the questions.

1. Which three states have apples as their top crop?

Washington   New Hampshire   West Virginia

2. The top crop for most states is _____
A. wheat
B. corn
C. soybeans
D. potatoes

3. What percentage of states grow wheat or corn as their top crop?
48 _____ %

4. Name three crops that are included in the category *Other* in the pie chart.
Answers will vary. _____ _____

5. Potatoes are the top crop grown in _____ of the states.
A. 8%
B. 12%
C. 18%
D. 6%

6. What is the top crop in your state?
Answers will vary.

7. Describe another way the information in the infographic could be presented.
Answers will vary.

162   The Visual Guide to Second Grade

Page 163

Make a Chart
In the chart below, show how many states grow each crop. For each crop, make a tally mark to show how many states grow it as their top crop. Count the tally marks in each row and write the total.

Examples:
| = 1 ||||| = 5 ||||| ||| = 8

Top Crop		Number of States	Total
Corn		||||| ||||| ||||| |||	18
Soybeans		||||| |||	8
Wheat		|||||		6
Fruit		||||| ||	7
Peanuts		||	2

Which crop is the top crop in the most states? _____ corn _____
Which crop is the top crop in the fewest states? _____ peanuts _____

Write About It

Meadowview Elementary School

Lunch Menu for Tuesday, September 23:

Peanut Butter and Grape Jelly Sandwich on Wheat Bread
Popcorn
Apple

Read the lunch menu. Where did the ingredients come from? Write about the states where the foods and ingredients might have been grown.
Answers will vary.

The Visual Guide to Second Grade   163

Page 166

Do the Math
Solve the problems. Use the infographic to help you.

1. In 1960, about how many gallons of gas could you buy for $1?
A. 1
B. 3
C. 5
D. 7

2. How much more was a gallon of gas in 1990 than in 1960?
$0.70

3. True or false? A pound of hamburger cost $1.25 in 1990.
False

4. Which cost more in 1990: two movie tickets or four pounds of hamburger?
two movie tickets

5. How much less did a small bag of popcorn cost in 1960 than in 2010?
$5.30

6. The cost of a gallon of gas _____ from 1990 to 2010.
A. more than doubled
B. went up by more than $2.00
C. stayed the same
D. fell

7. In 1990, how many movie tickets could you buy for $10.00?
2

166   The Visual Guide to Second Grade

Page 172

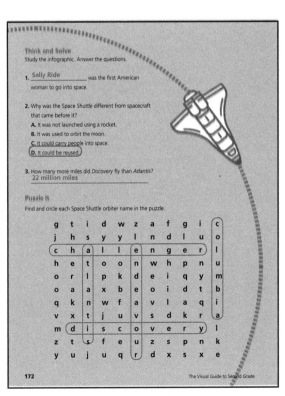

Think and Solve
Study the infographic. Answer the questions.

1. Sally Ride _____ was the first American woman to go into space.

2. Why was the Space Shuttle different from spacecraft that came before it?
A. It was not launched using a rocket.
B. It was used to orbit the moon.
C. It could carry people into space.
D. It could be reused.

3. How many more miles did *Discovery* fly than *Atlantis*?
22 million miles

Puzzle It
Find and circle each Space Shuttle orbiter name in the puzzle.

```
g  t  i  d  w  z  a  f  g  i  c
j  h  s  y  y  l  n  d  l  u  o
c  h  a  l  l  e  n  g  e  r  l
h  e  t  o  o  n  w  h  p  n  u
o  r  l  p  k  d  e  i  q  y  m
o  a  a  x  b  e  o  i  d  t  b
q  k  n  w  f  a  v  l  a  q  i
v  x  t  j  u  v  s  d  k  r  a
m  d  i  s  c  o  v  e  r  y  l
z  t  s  f  e  u  z  s  p  n  k
y  u  j  u  q  r  d  x  s  x  e
```

172   The Visual Guide to Second Grade

Page 173

Classify It

Read each fact. Circle *T* if it is true and *F* if it is false.

1. T (F) *Discovery* was the last Space Shuttle to go into space.
2. (T) F *Columbia* and *Challenger* both exploded.
3. T (F) The Space Shuttle program ended in 2000.
4. (T) F *Discovery* flew more miles than any other Space Shuttle.
5. (T) F *Endeavour's* name was chosen in a school competition.

Make a Bar Graph

Use the infographic to help you fill in the bar graph. Beside each orbiter name, draw a bar that shows how long the shuttle flew. Color each bar a different color.

Life of the Space Shuttle Orbiters

Atlantis	
Endeavour	
Discovery	
Columbia	
Challenger	

1980 1982 1984 1986 1988 1990 1992 1994 1996 1998 2000 2002 2004 2006 2008 2010 2012

Page 173

Page 176

Think and Solve

Study the infographic. Answer the questions.

1. True or false? Both Harriet and John Tubman were slaves.
   False

2. How old was Harriet when she married John?
   24 years old

3. An abolitionist is _____
   A. someone who is against slavery
   B. a slave who works on a farm
   C. a slave hunter
   D. someone who believes women should have the right to vote

Read About It: **What Harriet Said**

A *quotation*, or quote, tells exactly what someone said.
Read the quotes below by Harriet Tubman.

"I was the conductor of the Underground Railroad for eight years, and I can say what most conductors can't say — I never ran my train off the track and I never lost a passenger."

"There was no one to welcome me to the land of freedom. I was a stranger in a strange land."

"I grow up like a neglected weed — ignorant of liberty, having no experience of it."

"There was one of two things I had a right to, liberty, or death; if I could not have one, I would have the other."

Write About It

Choose one of the Harriet Tubman quotes above. What does it mean to you? Write your thoughts on the lines.

Answers will vary.

Page 176

Page 177

Sequence It

Imagine that a cousin sent you the note below giving instructions for using the Underground Railroad. Read the note. Then, number the steps below in the correct order.

> Cousin,
> Here is what you must to do to find your way to freedom. Save food in the days before you leave. Apples, hard-cooked eggs, bread—anything that will travel well. Wait for a moonless night. Walk through Briar's Creek for as long as you can. If there are dogs, they will not be able to track your scent.
> Head north to Wickets' farm. If there is a red shirt on the line, you can stay in the barn during the day. They will leave food for you in the last stall. Use the North Star to guide your way. You will come to a large wood. The trees will hide you during the day. When you reach the swamp, go around it. Too many dangers lie within. At the other side of the woods, you'll find a small cabin. When two candles flicker in the window, it is safe. Go around back, and you'll be told where to head next.
> You must commit this all to memory right away. Then destroy the note. It is not safe for you to keep.
> Good luck in your journey.
>
> Cousin Elijah

3   Head north to Wickets' farm.
6   Look for a small cabin with two candles in the window.
2   Walk through Briar's Creek.
1   Save food in the days before you leave.
4   Stay in the Wickets' barn during the day.
5   Go around the swamp.

Page 177